'HOW TO'
BOOK OF
CHOOSING & ENJOYING
WINE

ARTHUR BONE

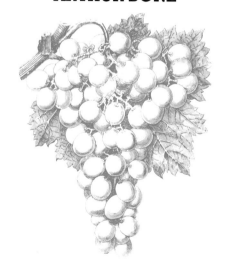

BLANDFORD PRESS
POOLE, DORSET

'HOW TO'

The 'How To' Book of Choosing and Enjoying Wine has been designed to present in the most lucid and straightforward terms the information which is essential to the buying, serving and drinking of table wines and fortified wines.

Contents

The 'How To' Book of Choosing and Enjoying
Wine was conceived, edited and
designed by Simon Jennings and Company Limited
42 Maiden Lane, London WC2, England

General Editor: Michael Bowers

Art Direction: Simon Jennings

Text: Arthur Bone

Illustrations: Stephen Bull, Jackson-Day Designs,
Carole Johnson, Susan Milne

Special Photography: John Couzins

Design & Research Assistant: Caroline Peacocke

First published in the United Kingdom 1981
Copyright © 1981 Blandford Press Limited
Link House, West Street, Poole,
Dorset BH15 1LL, England

Text and Illustrations Copyright
© 1981 Simon Jennings and Company Limited

ISBN 07137 1049 7
Printed in Singapore

THE AUTHOR
Arthur Bone had spent
many years in the wine
trade before playing a
leading part in the
establishment of an
education branch in the
Wine and Spirit
Association of Great
Britain. When,
subsequently, the Wine
and Spirit Education
Trust was formed as a
separate body, Arthur
Bone became its Director
of Studies – a post which
he still holds. His world-
wide experience of the
wine trade is second to
none, and he is the co-
author of two previous
books.

Introduction

Choosing and buying wine is a practical matter. Enjoyment depends upon making the right choice of style and quality and upon paying the right price – no wine will be totally satisfying if you have paid too much for it. Knowledge of wine, as of most things, comes with experience. To get that experience, however, choice has to be made – and that is where books become valuable. The practical value of this book lies in helping you to find your way around the vast assortment of wines on offer, and in helping you to choose according to your particular tastes and preferences.

As wine has become more universally available, some curious attitudes have grown up around it. On the one hand, the rich and ostentatious pay ever more fabulous sums for a few of the world's great wines – while ignoring others of equal quality. On the other, a vast amount of disgusting stuff is consumed by people for whom, apparently, cheapness is goodness. There is no merit in being able to buy poor wine cheaply. Neither is there any virtue in being able to afford Romanée-Conti – especially if you never buy anything else. Wine is not a cheap commodity, neither is it a necessary part of our diet (there are many who will dispute that), so there is no point in not treating it with a certain amount of respect and buying the best you can afford.

This book is a guide to the major producers of quality wines and to the wines they make. It tells you how to keep them, serve them, taste them and which foods go well with them. Above all, it tries to convey something useful about their qualities, but always with the assumption that you will want to try them rather than just read about them. It will help you to make an assessment of the rows of labels in your wine store and, if you are willing to experiment, it will rapidly increase the number of your favourite wines.

You will soon discover why it is that wine is a subject so much talked and written about; why there is so much romanticism wrapped around it, and why so many people devote their lives to growing it, making it, studying it – or just drinking it.

What is wine?

Wine is the fermented juice of the grape. Grape juice is rich in sugar and it is this sugar which converts into alcohol when it comes into contact with the yeast which forms on the skin of the ripening grape.

Although many other fruits, berries, vegetables etc., can be made to ferment and be turned into alcoholic drinks which are often called 'fruit wines' or 'country wines' it is the grape, and only the grape, which makes true wine.

The origins

The true origins of wine are not known, but it is reasonable to assume that primitive man soon learned the need to store some of the abundant fruits of summer to tide him over the bleak lean months of winter. If some of these fruits were wild grapes, perhaps stored in a hollow rock, they would ferment and the bubbling liquid would become wine.

The earliest records, however, show archaeological evidence of wine making in Asia-minor some 12,000 years ago. There is also ample evidence in Egyptian 'tomb paintings' of wine-making in Egypt some 2000 years BC.

Early wine makers
Wine has been important to mankind for a very long time, evidence of which is shown here by the pre-Christian relief of grape pickers, *below left*, and the medieval grape crushers, *below*. The latter, from a 14th Century manuscript in the British Library, depicts a scene that would be familiar in many parts of the world today The illustration from a 15th Century manuscript called "Le Rusticon", *right*, shows clearly how vines were trained 400 years ago. The vineyards in northern Italy, *top left*, and near Palermo in Sicily, *bottom right*, have probably been unchanged in appearance for centuries.

3,000 years of wine

As the Greek culture grew and as Greek sailors sailed around the Mediterranean, they were soon settling down and colonising places along the African, Italian and Iberian coastlines. The Egyptians soon found Greek wine more to their liking than their own. Heroditus, the Greek historian, writes on the export trade with Egypt and notes that, from all the wine shipped, none of the empty jars (*Amphorae*) were returned for re-filling. These amphorae were highly prized in southern Egypt to store water in the desert regions. The Greek amphorae were impervious and, if sealed with olive oil, were airtight. These sealed jars were to change wine from a mere beverage to wine that would keep fresh and mature over several years – a practice used by the Romans who made wines like *Falernium*, said to be at its best when 15–20 years old.

The Romans were great conquerors and marched north into new territories and, as the Empire spread, so did viticulture. It is to the Romans that most of the credit for European vineyards must be given and all of the great vineyard regions owe their original development to those in Europe.

Church influence

But the Romans came and they went: as the Empire shrunk and perished, it was Christianity that survived and with it, viticulture. Wine was necessary for the communion in the Christian Church, so it is easy to understand the interest taken by the religious brethren in wine production. Church influence in wine was considerable in medieval times

and vast areas of vineyard land were under its direct ownership. Many of these ecclesiastical properties remain today as the names of famous wines.

The Norman Conquest brought a change to English drinking habits. The Saxons were largely ale drinkers whilst the Normans drank wine. Ale houses, serving only ale, changed to taverns serving both ale and wine. Just over a century after the Norman invasion a certain Henry, Duke of Anjou, married Eleanor of Aquitaine thus uniting the great wine producing regions of the Loire and Bordeaux. So when Henry, just two years later, became Henry II of England this great wine producing sector of France came directly under the English crown and stayed so for some 300 years, until Joan of Arc forced the English to retreat. Trouble with France interfered with the supply of wine for some time and Britain turned to other sources of supply – chiefly Spain and Portugal.

Soon the colonies in Australia and South Africa started to produce wine and send it to the Homeland. The German influence on the Royal Family in Georgian and Victorian times brought Rhenish, the Hocks and Moselle into Britain and, in turn, America.

The all powerful vine
Dionysus, the Greek god of wine, was invariably portrayed, *right*, as a figure of power and authority. The vinestock, a rod surmounted by a sprig of vine leaves – carried here by one of Dionysus' attendants – became a symbol of authority much used by the Romans. Greek wine of the period, about 500 BC, would have been resinated – just as it is today.

How wine is grown

The quality of wine depends upon the skill of the maker and the quality of the grape harvest – the vintage. The quality of the vintage depends upon the skill of the grower and, ultimately, the weather. It is easy to forget that wine growing is a horticultural operation much like any other. The annual cycle, which for the vine begins in winter with pruning and taking of cuttings, includes all the tedious and time consuming, but vital, tasks that can be seen on any crop growing farm.

Soil cultivation, spraying, weeding, spraying again, thinning, more spraying, until the time comes in autumn to pick grapes that are perfect for wine making. Unless, of course, the weather has intervened. Frost, especially on young shoots in May, and hail are the chief destroyers of grapes. There are some frost protection measures available to growers, but there is no method of preventing a hail strike which could completely destroy the crop.

The ripeness of grapes is everything. A dry year, with constant warm sunshine, is likely to produce a good, even a great, vintage. A cold spring followed by a wet summer will produce unripe grapes, high in acidity and low in sugar.

Ancient and modern
Primitive methods are still
employed in some vineyards in
Italy, *above left*, but elsewhere
ultra modern equipment is
commonly seen. Spraying is
especially suited to mechanical
application, *below left* and
right. In earlier times,
according to the 'Book of
Trades' published in 1568,
below, "The vinegrower must
hack, dig, plant, prop, graft,
bind and prune in springtime in
order to have wine in autumn."

Der Rebmann.

Ich bin ein Hacker im Weinberg
Im Frůling hab ich harte werck/
Mit graben/ pålen vnd mit hauwen/
Mit Pfålstossn/ pflantzen vnd bauwen/
Mit auffbinden vnd schneiden die Reben/
Biß im Herbst die Trauben Wein geben:
Den man schneidt vnd außpreßt deñ fein
Noa erfand erstlich den Wein.
                    c iij   Der

11

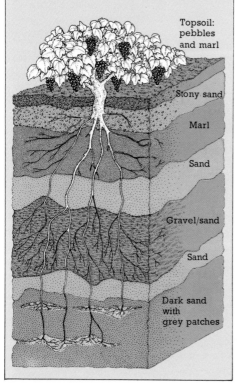

THE ANATOMY OF A VINE

This diagram shows how a vine in typical gravelly/sandy soil spreads its roots in the layers of nutritious marl and moisture containing gravel, but does not put out roots in compacted sand. The patches of grey sand contain water.

Topsoil: pebbles and marl

Stony sand

Marl

Sand

Gravel/sand

Sand

Dark sand with grey patches

Cultivation & climate

Nature has provided, in the form of grapes, the most perfect 'do-it-yourself' winemaking kit. The flesh of the grape contains all the essential ingredients of wine; water, sugar, acids and a variety of trace elements. The skins contain not only the pigments which colour the wine, but also the millions of tiny organisms, called *yeasts*, which are the agents of fermentation – which turns grape juice into wine. The essence of successful wine making is the correct choice of grape and the balancing and control of natural processes. The two factors which most affect the grower in his choice of grape, in any wine growing region, are soil and climate.

Soil

Because the roots of the vine go down some 20–30 feet you will see that it is not just the topsoil but also several layers of subsoil that will influence the crop. Trace elements of the chemicals and mineral salts in the soil will be sucked up by the roots and deposited in the grapes and will be passed on to become flavour in the wine. It is often the poor soils which make the fine wines of great character, while rich alluvial soil tends to make more ordinary wines, lacking finesse and tasting rather flat and flabby.

It is not just the chemical contents of the soil but also its physical properties that affect the grapes. In Champagne for example, the soil is solid chalk. Chalk, which is alkaline, produces a rather acid wine, and it is this acidity which helps to make Champagne the great wine that it is – often referred to as the 'King of Wine and the Wine of Kings'. A thousand miles away in Jerez, where sherry is made, the soil is also chalky, not solid chalk but with a high chalk content. Although Champagne and Sherry are poles apart, the great Fino Sherries also have a marked acidity which helps to make them a wine for the connoisseur. The great Clarets of Bordeaux are grown on poor gravelly soil and yet turn out to be some of the world's finest red wines. In Germany, the fine delicate Moselle wine is made from grapes grown on broken flakes of slate. Up in the Douro hills, the grapes grow in heavy granitic and shistous rock – yet the wine made from these grapes becomes Port, the finest of which will still be drunk and enjoyed perhaps 50 years later.

CLIMATIC ZONES

The vine, like all plants, has some preference as to where it grows. The conditions which suit it best are to be found in two bands across the world, between (roughly) 30° and 50° north and south of the Equator. Between these latitudes grapes ripen adequately – which means that they contain enough sugar and a balanced acidity.

Even within the acceptable limits of latitude the effects can vary considerably. The general climate may be distorted, moderated or exaggerated by the proximity of the sea, inland lakes, hills, mountains and forests. All of this can create micro climates, or zones within zones, where the vine can excel, and if these coincide with an area of very suitable soil it is only necessary to select the correct and matching variety of vine.

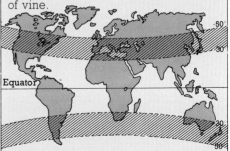

13

Selecting the grape

There are several species of the vine, but only *Vitis Vinifera*, the European species, is suitable to make wine. Within the species, there are dozens of varieties and these too must match the soil and climate to give of their best. The many varieties fall into just two types: black and white. The black or, to be more precise, red to deep purple, grapes have a juice which is as white as the pale skinned grapes: the colouring matter is only in the skins. Their significance in making the wine is that red wine can only be made from the black grapes but white wine can be made from either black or white grapes.

Grenache

Syrah

Riesling

Cabernet Sauvignon

Gewürztraminer

Pinot Noir

Semillon

Chardonnay

GRAPE VARIETIES

Grenache
The principal grape in Chateauneuf-du-Pape.
Syrah
Very dark, bitter grapes used in Hermitage and Côte Rôtie.
Cabernet Sauvignon
The chief grape in the making of Claret.
Semillon
A delicate grape used in the making of Sauternes.
Riesling
The chief white grape of Germany, Eastern Europe.
Gewürztraminer
Much used in Alsace where it makes powerful spicy wine.
Pinot Noir
The great grape of Burgundy – now much used elsewhere.
Chardonnay
The grape which produces the great white Burgundies.

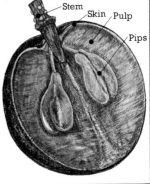

Stem · Skin · Pulp · Pips

15

How wine is made

When the grapes have been picked they are brought into the press house where they are fed into a crusher. The crusher, in addition to preparing the grapes for fermentation, removes the stems and passes the juicy mixture into the press. At this point, the process takes a slightly different course for each colour of wine. White grapes have their skins removed, but black grapes on the way to becoming red wine will ferment with their skins. If their skins were taken away, the resulting wine would be white. Rosé is produced by separating the juice from the skins of red grapes after a short period of fermentation.

The need to control fermentation is brought about by the activities of the yeasts and bacteria which cause it to happen. There are two main types of yeast: wild yeasts and wine yeasts. There are many other moulds and bacteria present on the skins of grapes, but only the *aceter bacter*, or vinegar bacteria, is of any importance.

FERMENTATION

The wild yeasts start the fermentation but produce only 4% of alcohol and an 'off' taste in the wine. The wine yeasts then take over, converting the rest of the sugar to about 10% of alcohol, and then the vinegar bacteria will turn the wine into vinegar. This is obviously not what is wanted – the natural process must be controlled. In controlled fermentation, the unwanted wild yeasts and vinegar bacteria must be eliminated to allow the wine yeasts to produce the whole 10% of alcohol without contamination. Temperature plays a part and the wine maker can use it to alter the speed of the fermentation. The yeasts, which are tiny living organisms, can only exist within a temperature range of 4–32°C (40–90°F). The closer the temperature is to the cold end the slower they work; the nearer they are to the hot end the faster they work. A short sharp fermentation is more suitable for producing light, inexpensive, wine but a long fermentation will produce a finer wine.

WINE MAKING THE BASIC PROCESS

WHITE WINE

●

White wine can be made from red or white grapes.

●

The grapes are first put into a crusher-stemmer which breaks them and removes the stalks.

●

The broken grapes are then fed into a cylindrical press.

●

The press revolves and a steel screw pushes the ends together. Juice runs out into a trough and the skins are left in the press.

●

Juice is then pumped into the fermenting vat where its fermenting time is determined by the type of wine required.

Sweet wine
Can be made by stopping the fermentation before all the sugar is converted into alcohol. Usually this is done by adding sulphur or filtering out the yeasts.

Dry wine
This is achieved by allowing fermentation to continue until all the sugar has been converted.

Sparkling wine
Can be made in a number of ways, but the most natural is to bottle the wine before fermentation is complete – so that it continues in bottle.

RED WINE

●

Only red (black) grapes can be used in the making of red wine.

●

The grapes are put into a crusher but are not always de-stemmed (the stems increase the tannin content of wine).

●

After crushing, the grapes go straight into the fermenting vat with their skins – it is the skins that give the wine its colour. Fermentation continues until all sugar has been used (this takes about two weeks).

●

The wine is run off without any pressing and goes straight into barrels – to mature for whatever period is necessary for the style of wine.

●

The wine which remains with the skins, i.e. the wine which does not run off freely, is pressed out and blended with 'free run' wine to make an acceptable product. Press wine is naturally dark and bitter.

Marc
This is the remains of skins, pips and stems after pressing. It can be distilled to make cheap brandy, but is more frequently used as a fertilizer.

ROSÉ (PINK) WINE

●

Red grapes are used to make pink wines.

●

As before, the grapes are fed into a crusher (usually a crusher-stemmer).

●

The crushed grapes go into the fermenting vat with their skins and the process continues for a few days just as it does for red wine.

●

Once the wine has taken on a certain amount of colour, it is run off into another vat – leaving the skins behind. It then continues its fermentation in the usual way.

Pink wines are usually dry, but they can be sweet, or even sparkling.

The importance of age

For commercial reasons, most wine is bottled soon after the process of fermentation is complete. Some, like Beaujolais, is favoured by those wine drinkers who like to be fashionable when it is only weeks old. All wine, however, benefits from a period of maturation – however short.

The extent to which a wine is kept, either before bottling or in bottle, depends very largely on its capacity for improvement. Generally, one could say that the finer the wine the longer it may be allowed to mature, although individual wines and vintages will vary greatly in the extent to which they improve with age.

In the châteaux of Bordeaux no wine is bottled until it has been in barrels for two years. It is generally accepted that this is the minimum time required by the elements of a good wine to sort themselves out and begin to settle into the characteristic style of the wine. The effects of the oak in which the wine is kept, and the greater exposure to oxygen which one aged in barrels receives, are likely to make the wine more complex, subtle, intriguing and satisfying than a wine bottled after six weeks.

Time and maturity

Wine needs time for a variety of different reasons. Some, like Port, mature in wooden barrels which are made of oak. The barrels, called 'pipes' are made in the age-old way, *bottom right*, and new wine is always put into new wood. Burgundy, *top left*, spends much less time in wood but is still much affected by the period during which it is in cask – exposed to a small amount of oxygen. Champagne, *bottom left*, is bottled during its secondary fermentation and kept upside down until the process is complete. Other wines may go to a modern bottling plant, *below*, after only a few weeks, while Valdepeñas, *right*, is fermented in stone jars which are designed to admit oxygen.

Bottling & labelling

Many fine wines, because they are produced in relatively small quantities and bottled at source, are still bottled by hand or, at best, put through a small and simple machine bottling line. Large productions, however, are handled on quite sophisticated bottling machines with a multiplicity of functions.

Besides these essential functions of filling, inserting the cork, covering the cork and labelling, many modern systems have additional facilities. Bottle-washing, sterilizing and drying units may precede the filler but today most bottlers use new bottles supplied already sterile in shrink-wrapped plastic packs ready for use. After 'dressing' the bottles are usually packed into cases or cartons. Fine wines are often wrapped in tissue paper and a wooden case is still used for great château Clarets, Vintage Port and a few others. Even so, the corrugated cardboard carton, with divisions for a dozen bottles, has become today's standard wine pack. Twelve is still the quantity unit in the wine trade and looks like staying, because a pack of ten makes a very awkward shape.

Quality control

Behind the whole operation are two very important people. First, the Wine Taster, whose job it is to select the wines for their style, quality and taste. Secondly, the Quality Controller, who is responsible for checking the wine on receiving it from the supplier and at each stage of the operation to ensure perfection. He will test the wine in his laboratory for a variety of things, like alcohol, acidity, sugar etc., which are natural components of wine but appear in varying quantities. He will also test for unnatural things like contaminations or infections. As part of his control he may order special handling for some wines and perhaps even a procedure more likely to be found in a hospital than a factory. Sterile bottling is often used for light delicate wines, like some of the German wines, which are low in alcohol but contain some residual sugar and are therefore rather susceptible to yeast infection. A section of the cellar is partitioned off so that a very high standard of hygiene can be maintained. The bottles are sterilized immediately before the filler and a flame passes over the lip of the bottle before a sterilized cork is driven in.

Labels

Comparatively new EEC legislation has standardised the labelling law for all light wines produced in or imported into and offered for sale in the EEC. Laws for Sparkling and Heavy (Fortified) wine are expected to follow soon. This means that only objective information now appears on the label; some is optional but some is compulsory.

Distinctions are made between EEC and Non EEC wine and between quality and non quality wine. The Country of Origin, the name and address of the Bottler and the volume of contents in cl. is required information.

Italian Labels

There was a time when Italian labels would contain a good deal of fanciful verbiage and not much useful information. The EEC has changed that, although romantic and colourful images still abound. Now, however, the regional name of the wine is given more prominence than was the case a few years ago.

READING THE LABEL

The meaning of a typical Bordeaux label

1 The name of the wine – in this case, it is the name of the vineyard.
2 Classification: this is one of the second great growths (Grand Cru) of the Medoc.
3 The Appellation Contrôlée district – St. Julien is in the Medoc.
4 The name of the grower.
5 The place of bottling (in this case, the vineyard) and the date of vintage.
6 The name of the merchant who bought the wine and kept it until it was shipped.
7 The contents of the bottle, in centilitres.

See pages 39–44

Bottle recognition

Whilst bottles come in all shapes and sizes it has been traditional for many years for certain shapes to be associated with special regions.

Because there are far too many wines for each to have a special design one will always find Claret in a Claret bottle and Hock in a Hock bottle, but conversely not all Claret shaped bottles will contain Claret and not all Hock-shaped bottles will contain Hock. The colour of the glass may also be important and will vary from clear glass through a range of amber to brown and green – which might also be in varying depth of colour according to the bottle manufacturing country or company.

Bottle shapes
The bottles shown here were all developed for the wines illustrated. There are many other shapes, both traditional and fanciful, and many variations of colour and capacity. In general, however, standard bottles will contain between 70 and 75cl of wine.

CAPSULE
NECK
NECK LABEL
SHOULDER
LABEL
BACK LABEL
PUNT

Bordeaux Red

Bordeaux White

Burgundy

A dark green bottle with well-defined shoulders.

Always clear revealing the depth of colour in the wine.

White and red use a similar shape and colour.

Loire

Alsace

Rhein

Port

A shape used for many white and red wines in this region.

Taller than German bottles but similar in design.

Rhein wines have brown glass, Moselles are green.

The traditional shape – ideal for laying down.

Classifying wine

Basically, wine is classified into three main groups; ordinary simple wine which has no quality status; quality wine which conforms to certain laid down standards and usually confined to a region of origin, and super quality wine – conforming to the quality status but having additional special attributes accredited to it.

Whilst most of the major commercial producing countries have their own and varying systems of quality control, most fall loosely into the three tier pattern, although the approach may be very different from one country to another, and from one region to another. In France, for instance, the system works roughly as follows: there is ordinary wine which can come into the categories *vin ordinaire* or *vin de Pays*; both are non-quality wines but vin de Pays is one that has the privilege of adding a geographical status, usually the department. There are two tiers of quality wine, *Vin Délimité de Qualité Supérieure* (VDQS for short), which contains middle quality wines, and *Appellation d'Origine Contrôlée* which includes the top quality wines which have to conform to rigid standards and to be produced within a controlled

zone. But even these AOC wines can have degrees of importance. These in ascending order of importance, would be *region, area, village* or *vineyard*.

In Germany they also have three groups, *Tafelwein* or non-quality wine, *Qualitätswein - bestimmte - Anbaugebiete* (QbA) which is ordinary quality, plus the super quality *Qualitätswein-mit-Prädikat* (QmP). Prädikaten are special attributes relating to the additional ripeness of the grapes used.

Italy also has a three tier system of simple non-quality wines and quality wines, *Denominazione d'Origine Controllata* (DOC).

The meaning of quality

These, of course, are the basic requirements of law in the classification of wine. The average wine drinker more often wants to know the precise difference between wines described as 'ordinary' (vin ordinaire, vin de pays), 'good' and 'fine'. Ordinary wines vary greatly in quality, the only rules (where they exist) governing strength. Good, on the other hand, presupposes quality – but not all quality wines would be considered good by the expert. The situation can be rather complicated. In

France, some *Appellation Contrôlée* areas regularly produce wine, below individual vineyard status, which have all the right characteristics of their type and region and may be considered good. On the other hand, it is possible to find many classed growths and other château or estate bottled wines which are no better. In general, however, the wines which are known by the name of their vineyard and are bottled on the premises, are most likely to be the fine wines.

The same can be said of Germany, but there are few other countries where there is so much certainty.

In Italy, where there used to be more confusion than there is now, it would be hard to generalise. The best thing to do is learn which are supposed to be the good and fine wines – then try them.

In Spain it is a matter of knowing the reputable brand names, both for sherries and Riojas. The same can be said for Port and all the fortified áperitif and dessert wines – they are all subject to a different system of classification. Quality control is now a matter of prime concern in wine making throughout the world, and the base level of quality is being raised considerably.

FINE WINES

Fame and fashion
The finest wines tend to suffer the disadvantages of fame. Those with a reputation for greatness, such as the Châteaux of Lafite and Latour, are unreasonably expected to make great wine from every vintage – and they are priced as if they do. The Königin Victoria Berg, below left, was one of the most fashionable and expensive wines during the 19th century. Although it still makes top quality wine, it is no longer fashionable and can be bought at moderate prices.

25

Fortified wines

A fortified wine is one which has had brandy or alcohol added. This form of adulteration is necessary to the production of Sherry, Port, Madeira, Malaga and Marsala. The brandy stops fermentation, strengthens the wine and, except in the case of Sherry, preserves a proportion of the natural grape sugar. In sherry production, the addition of brandy comes too late in the process to preserve the sugar, so the wines have to be sweetened – even some of the very dry ones.

In most cases, these wines are the results of blending as well as fortifying. In all cases, the unprocessed wines would be inferior and probably unpalatable. The great aperitif and dessert wines, therefore, mostly came into being because ways had to be found to make vast quantities of poor quality wine saleable. Centuries of refinement and development have given us wines which are the perfect before- and after-dinner drinks. More than that, they have been responsible for a good deal of ritual, romanticism and inspiration. The delicacy and austerity of a fino Sherry, the elegance and well-being of an old tawny Port, the luxuriant sweetness of a Malmsey are quite unique.

Growing and blending

The making of Sherry and Port is a long and carefully controlled process in which many experts and craftsmen are involved. The Sherry growers, *top left*, inspecting new vines, and the taster assessing the blended wine, *below left*, are specialists in a highly developed science. Sherry is made in Bodegas, similar to the one shown here, *right*, where the juice from the Palomino grapes, *below* is fermented and blended. These grapes, *bottom*, have to be carried down sheer slopes in baskets – as they have for centuries.

Storage and care

The world produces annually something between seven and eight thousand million gallons of wine; the precise figure is difficult to ascertain because much is produced by small farmers for their own consumption. Something in the region of 80% is red wine and the remainder mostly white, rosé being a very tiny proportion, and most of it is ordinary everyday drinking wine and therefore stored only long enough for practical purposes.

A cellar under the house is the ideal place for wine storage because the temperature will remain fairly steady around 55°F or 14°C but, as most modern houses do not have this luxury, a cupboard, preferably in the centre of the house where the temperature is more constant, will do. Do not store more than you have to, but it is important to note that fine wines are cheaper when bought young and stored until mature. The bottles should be laid down to keep the corks moist and be kept as near as possible to a 'cellar' temperature. Racks are useful for storage because individual bottles are separated and easy to identify but, if these are unobtainable, carefully planned shelves or boxes can be used.

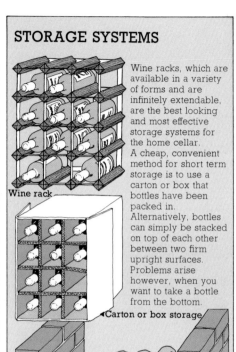

STORAGE SYSTEMS

Wine racks, which are available in a variety of forms and are infinitely extendable, are the best looking and most effective storage systems for the home cellar.
A cheap, convenient method for short term storage is to use a carton or box that bottles have been packed in.
Alternatively, bottles can simply be stacked on top of each other between two firm upright surfaces. Problems arise however, when you want to take a bottle from the bottom.

Wine rack

Carton or box storage

Self-stacking method

28

Good wines, particularly red wines, respond very well to careful storage over periods from two to even fifty years. Of course, it is important to point out that only the very finest of the good wines will last for twenty years or more, and these great wines are a very tiny proportion – even of wines given quality status. In France, the greatest fine wine producing country, only about 20% are given quality status. Most wine, therefore, is bottled for immediate consumption and, apart from having a few bottles to hand, needs no special storage.

Most white wines and rosés are best drunk young while they are fresh and fruity – only a very few rather special whites need laying down to mature. Fine white Burgundies, luscious Sauternes and Auslese and Beerenauslese are the ones for keeping.

Most red wines, because of their tannin content, will improve with keeping for short periods even though they are bottled for immediate consumption.

Fine Clarets, Burgundies, Rhône wines and some fine Italian and Spanish wines will keep for much longer periods, but they must be well selected.

STORAGE

Any domestic cupboard, especially the built-in sort with ventilated doors, can be turned into an effective wine store. It should not be in a very warm part of the house, nor where the temperature varies a great deal. Buy, or make, racks to fit and make use of any available shelves to store related pieces of equipment – wine baskets, decanting funnels, corkscrews.

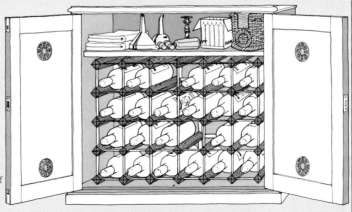

Champagne

It is less than 100 years since Champagne pushed its way into the general consciousness as the great wine for celebrations and special occasions. During that time, Champagne has become a byword for style, sophistication and elegance. Consequently, the name itself has come in for a good deal of misuse, and the associations which most of us instantly make when Champagne is mentioned probably do the wine less than justice. True, it is now the most popular drink at weddings, ceremonial occasions and many other gregarious assemblies, but it is never appreciated under those circumstances as it really ought to be. Champagne, like Sherry and Port, has a long history of refinement and improvement and is not merely a sparkling wine with a better reputation than the others.

Champagne is another blended wine and the secret of a good one is the delicate and subtle balance which is achieved between the unmistakable flavour of fruit, the natural acidity derived from the chalk soil of the region and the peculiarly stimulating qualities of the wine. The complexities of Champagne demand a clean palate and time to savour its depths.

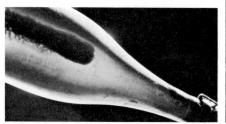

Growing and blending
Champagne is made from both
black and white grapes, the
Pinot Noir, *right*, being as
important as the Chardonnay.
Champagne country has rich
but thin soil. The subsoil,
below, is a thick seam of chalk
which gives the wine its acidity.
Blending, *top left*, is
carried out by the Chefs de
Cave – men who have a
lifetime's experience of the
Champagne taste. During the
secondary fermentation of the
wine, a cloudy sediment is
formed in the bottle, *bottom
left*. This is later removed.
see pages 59–60

Serving wine

The first essential is to be sure that the wine you intend to serve has been stored well and is in good condition. Always plan ahead, allowing plenty of time for chilling or decanting. Although few wines need decanting, there are many that will benefit from being able to breathe for a while before consumption.

The only necessary equipment in the serving of wine is a corkscrew and suitable glasses. There may be other bits and pieces which will enhance the service, but none is essential.

Temperature

The following chart provides a simple guide to the serving of most wines.

TEMPERATURE	WINES
40–45 F 5–7 C	Sparkling wines; sweet white wines
46–52 F 8–11 C	Alsace, Chablis and ordinary dry white; rosé; dry Sherry
53–55 F 12–13 C	Other Sherries; light red wines; white Port
56–62 F 14–17 C	Most red wines; Port; Madeira; fine white Burgundy
63–66 F 17–19 C	Finest red wines: Bordeaux, Burgundy Hermitage, Barolo etc.

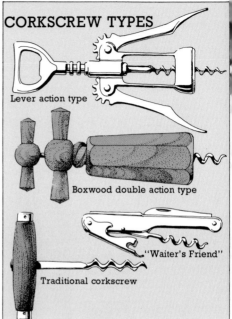

CORKSCREW TYPES

Lever action type

Boxwood double action type

"Waiter's Friend"

Traditional corkscrew

Worm thread

Corkscrew types

The lever action is an excellent type for removing sound, even tough, corks – but it may split a weak one. The double-action type is probably the best, but check that it sits neatly on the lip of the bottle. The folding type with lever and blade is extremely uncomfortable to use, but the traditional corkscrew, with a worm thread – not a gimlet or solid core – is still one of the most reliable.

Some old wines throw a sediment as they mature, which is quite natural, but the wine should be allowed to settle and then be decanted leaving a small amount of wine (with the sediment) in the bottle so that the decanted wine is bright and clean when it is served. Usually, white wines are served much younger than red and therefore rarely need decanting. It is usually old and fine red wines like Claret, Burgundy and Vintage Port that come into these decanting categories. The equipment required, besides the corkscrew, consists of a clear glass decanter, a candle and a glass. The only other essential, of course, is a steady hand. Making sure that the shoulder of the bottle is clean enough for you to see through take the bottle in the right hand and the decanter in the left, hold the neck of the bottle over the candle and gently start to pour, watching for the sediment rising to the shoulder and neck of the bottle. Stop pouring when it reaches this level. Some big robust wines like Barolo from Northern Italy, are worth decanting even if they have no sediment as this tends to aerate the wine and bring out the bouquet.

HOW TO DECANT WINE

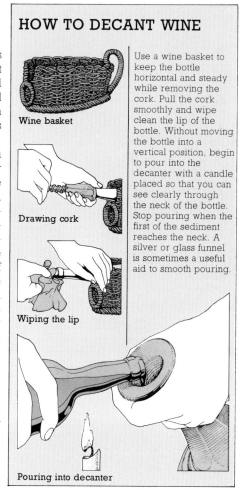

Wine basket

Drawing cork

Wiping the lip

Pouring into decanter

Use a wine basket to keep the bottle horizontal and steady while removing the cork. Pull the cork smoothly and wipe clean the lip of the bottle. Without moving the bottle into a vertical position, begin to pour into the decanter with a candle placed so that you can see clearly through the neck of the bottle. Stop pouring when the first of the sediment reaches the neck. A silver or glass funnel is sometimes a useful aid to smooth pouring.

Wine glasses

Although it can be argued that wine is still wine whatever it is served in, it is important to appreciate it with the eye and nose as well as the tongue. Wine is, therefore, greatly enhanced by being served in thin, clear, uncoloured glasses. They should be big enough to contain a reasonable amount when only half-full and they should narrow slightly towards the top to hold the bouquet. It is not necessary to have special glasses for each wine, but there are some traditional shapes which have been evolved for certain wines and will present them to their best advantage. Some of them are shown here.

GLASS SHAPES

Of the glasses shown here, most were designed for specific wines. But two, the Tulip and the Paris goblet, are general purpose glasses. The Tulip is suitable for almost anything, including sparkling wines – but the Paris goblet is really a red wine glass.

Looking after glass
Clean glasses with hot water and no detergent. Dry them with clean cloths and store them upright. It is important to let air circulate in glasses and decanters while they are not in use, or they may take on unpleasant odours.

Paris goblet

Rhein (Hock)

Port/Madeira

Anjou (Loire)

Tulip

Sherry copita

Champagne flute

Alsace

WINES OF THE WORLD REGION BY REGION

The following pages provide a guide to the main producing regions of the world with special reference to wines which are generally available, i.e. with distribution not confined to the country of origin. The principal producers of quality wines, France, Germany and Italy, are dealt with region-by-region.

FRANCE

France is undoubtedly the World's greatest wine producing country. Italy may produce more, but only France has such a range of quality and fine wines. Even so, 75% of French wine is ordinary; VDQS accounting for approximately 5% and AC for 20%.

France not only has the longest history of stringent quality control in wine production, it also has a far greater wealth of tradition and romanticism associated with the vine. Partly, this is due to the fact that the wine growing regions, the Gironde, Dordogne, the Loire, Provence, the Midi, Burgundy, Champagne and Alsace, are so full of beautiful landscapes, idyllic villages and wonderful food. But it owes as much to geography, topography, climate and soil conditions. France is a big country, by European standards, and contains an unparalleled variety of soils and micro-climates which are perfect for growing the vine.

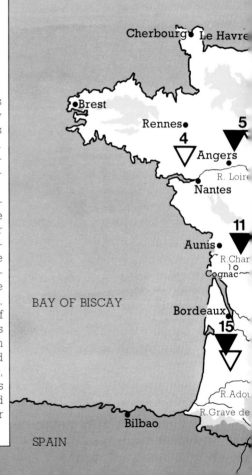

Cherbourg Le Havre

•Brest

Rennes•

4 5

Angers

R. Loire

Nantes

11

Aunis•

R.Char
lo
Cognac

BAY OF BISCAY

Bordeaux

15

R.Adou

R.Grave de

Bilbao

SPAIN

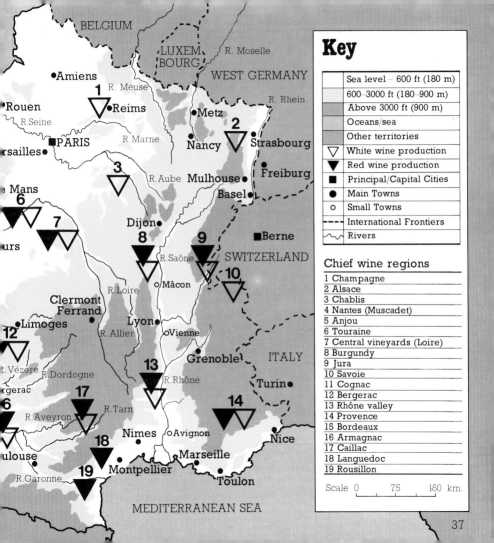

Key

	Sea level – 600 ft (180 m)
	600–3000 ft (180–900 m)
	Above 3000 ft (900 m)
	Oceans/sea
	Other territories
▽	White wine production
▼	Red wine production
■	Principal/Capital Cities
●	Main Towns
○	Small Towns
---	International Frontiers
∿	Rivers

Chief wine regions

1 Champagne
2 Alsace
3 Chablis
4 Nantes (Muscadet)
5 Anjou
6 Touraine
7 Central vineyards (Loire)
8 Burgundy
9 Jura
10 Savoie
11 Cognac
12 Bergerac
13 Rhône valley
14 Provence
15 Bordeaux
16 Armagnac
17 Caillac
18 Languedoc
19 Rousillon

Scale 0   75   150 km.

THE QUALITY WINES OF FRANCE

REGION	TYPES OF WINE	COMMENTS
BORDEAUX	Fine red wines; sweet white; dry white; some rosé	Château bottled red wines tend to be expensive and need time to mature; the world's best sweet wines come from Sauternes and Barsac. *Value tip:* *Cru Bourgeois and wines from Fronsac, Bourg and Blaye.*
BURGUNDY	Light to medium weight red wines; dry white	Red Burgundy is scarce and very pricy, even the humbler wines are not cheap; the equivalent quality in white wines is much cheaper. *Value tip:* *Wines from Maconnais, Chalonnais.*
LOIRE	Red; white – sweet, dry and sparkling; rosé	Very big range of styles and tastes – mostly good value. Excellent, but expensive, sweet wines. *Value tip:* *Vouvray, Coteaux du Layon, Savennieres.*
ALSACE	White – almost exclusively dry, but some sweet after long hot summers	Delicate spicy wines made from Riesling and Gewürztraminer grapes, also some Sylvaner and dry Muscat. There have been disappointments in recent years. *Value tip:* *Any wine from reputable growers.*
RHONE	Medium to weighty reds; dry white, sweet white; rosé	Wines with great depth, richness and long life. Some rare and expensive whites. Côtes du Rhône sometimes disappointing. *Value tip:* *Crozes-Hermitage, Gigondas, Tavel.*
CHAMPAGNE	White – mostly sparkling; some rosé and red	The finest of all sparkling wines. *Value tip:* *Buy the best you can afford.*

Bordeaux

The wine growing area is centred on the confluence of the rivers Dordogne and Garonne which flow, as the Gironde, into the Bay of Biscay. In this region, some 110km long and 25–35km wide, are grown some of the greatest of all red wines and sweet white wines.

The whole area is made up of some 15 districts, each with its own Appellation Contrôlée. The biggest districts, Graves and Entre-deux-Mers, produce sufficient white wine to ensure that Bordeaux is responsible for more white than red. Graves, however, makes much better red wine and, with the exception of Sauternes, it is the red (claret) which has established the greatness of Bordeaux.

In all the claret growing districts the method of wine making is meticulous. New wine is always put into new barrels and is 'racked off' (transferred to new casks) several times in the ensuing months to clear the wine of the rapidly-forming sediment. The wine will remain in barrels for at least two years.

It is bottled, very often by hand, usually in January or February when activity in the vineyard is at its lowest. Good clarets need at least 10 years in bottle to mature.

ABOUT CLARET

There have been vineyards in the Bordeaux district since Roman times, but it was not until that part of France fell into English hands during medieval times that Bordeaux wine became an export commodity. The English were most particular in their choice of wine and elaborate measures were taken to ensure that no adulterated wines got into the consignments awaiting shipment to England. The genuine wine, which was a marvellously clear, pale red, was called ''clairet'' – a word which was soon transformed into ''claret'' by the English. Since then, the word has become synonymous with the colour as much as with the wine and is used throughout the English-speaking world.

The Medoc

The Médoc makes only red wine and is the home of the most illustrious vineyards. In 1855, it was decided to produce a system of classifying the wines from the best Châteaux and to call them Grand Cru (Great Growths). The system is still in use today.

When it was instituted, the classification was based on the prices paid for quality wines. In 1855, this may have been a reliable indication of outstanding quality at the highest level – certainly Châteaux Lafite, Latour and Margaux have made the very finest clarets from time to time. Today, classed growths consistently achieve high prices but quality may be more erratic. Some third and fourth growths may produce greater wines than first or second growths, and some Cru Bourgeois – the group immediately below the classed growths – regularly make wine of a higher standard.

Value for money is most likely to be achieved by looking for well-reputed Cru Bourgeois from the areas of the four great wine growing villages of the Médoc: Pauillac, Margaux, St. Estéphe and St. Julien. To define the taste and character of claret is impossible without making a comparison of many different districts within the whole region. Claret is a wine of such subtlety and variety that it can change considerably in a distance of a few kilometres. For example: Pauillac, which is generally considered to make the finest wines, achieves the ideal balance between solidity and delicacy, between fruitiness and scent. The colour of Pauillac wines is brilliant enough to make anybody sit up and take notice. Pauillac's neighbour, St. Estéphe makes much 'bigger' and stronger flavoured wines while Margaux, in the southern Médoc, is known for its delicacy and perfume. The wine from St. Julien is smooth but less strikingly dry than many clarets.

It is easy enough for the inexperienced wine drinker to make these comparisons for himself – good wines from this region are easily available – but he should start out expecting claret to be light in colour, dry and refreshing. It often gives the impression of being tough if it is too young but will always improve with age. It is a very amenable wine, at its best with food, especially red meats, but also capable of warming on a winter day or cooling and reviving on a hot summer afternoon.

THE 1855 CLASSIFICATION OF THE MEDOC

PREMIER GRAND CRUS	First great growths	
Château Lafite-Rothschild Château Latour	Château Margaux Château Mouton-Rothschild	Château Haut-Brion (Graves)
DEUXIÈMES GRAND CRUS	*Second great growths*	
Château Rausan-Ségla Château Rauzan-Gassies Château Léoville-Las Cases Château Léoville-Poyferré Château Léoville-Barton	Château Durfort-Vivens Château Lascombes Château Gruaud-Larose Château Brane-Cantenac Château Pichon-Longueville	Château Pichon-Longueville (Comtesse de La Lande) Château Ducru-Beaucaillou Château Cos d'Estournel Château Montrose
TROISÈMES GRAND CRUS	*Third great growths*	
Château Kirwan Château d'Issan Château Lagrange Château Langoa Château Giscours	Château Malescot St-Exupéry Château Cantenac Brown Château Palmer Château la Lagune Château Desmirail	Château Calon Ségur Château Ferrière Château Marquis d'Alesme-Becker Château Boyd Cantenac
QUATRIÈMES CRUS	*Fourth great growths*	
Château St-Pierre Bontemps Château St-Pierre Sevaistre Château Branaire Ducru Château Talbot	Château Duhart Milon Château Pouget Château La Tour Carnet Château Rochet	Château Beychevelle Château le Prieuré-Lichine Château Marquis de Terme
CINQUIÈMES GRAND CRUS	*Fifth great growths*	
Château Pontet-Canet Château Batailley Château Haut-Batailley Château Grand Puy Lacoste Château Grand Puy Ducasse Château Lynch Bages	Château Lynch Moussas Château Dauzac Château Baron Philippe Château Le Tertre Château Haut Bages Liberal Château Pedesclaux	Château Belgrave Château Camensac Château Clos Labory Château Clerc-Milon Château Croizet-Bages Château Cantemerle

Pomerol & St Emilion

These towns lie further inland and on the other side of the river Dordogne; like the Médoc they produce only red wine. The wines are softer and gentler than those of the Médoc, but it is a round, rich softness – full of flavour and developing the balance of mature wine earlier than other clarets.

Pétrus

Château Pétrus, in Pomerol is one of the world's very finest red wines and has recently become one of the most expensive. Indeed, if the classification of 1855 were to be re-assessed the authorities would be obliged, if they operated on the same principles, to include Pétrus as a first growth, just as they did Château Haut-Brion in the first classification. Pomerols tend to be darker than most Bordeaux wines, and their rich, smooth and satisfying characteristics make them very easy drinking. They are made using the Merlot as the chief grape variety – a grape which is only of secondary importance in the rest of the Bordeaux region. This is also the principal grape in St. Emilion, whose wines are also rich, rounded and amenable. The best vineyard of St. Emilion is Château Cheval Blanc.

Graves

Graves produces a great deal of wine half of which is white, and it is the white that most people would associate with the district. It cannot even approach the quality of the red wine, however, but the red can challenge the best of the Médoc. When the classification of 1855 was worked out, the merchants who devised it were obliged to include Château Haut-Brion in the very highest category. Today, Châteaux La Mission-Haut-Brion, Smith-Haut-Lafitte Haut-Bailly and the Domaine de Chevalier are almost as good.

There is good value to be had from many of the minor Châteaux of the district – their wines not being much sought after – but they can be hard to track down.

1971

CHATEAU HAUT-BRION
PREMIER GRAND CRU CLASSÉ
APPELLATION GRAVES CONTRÔLÉE
MIS EN BOUTEILLES AU CHATEAU
DOMAINE CLARENCE DILLON S.A., A PESSAC, GIRONDE
MARQUE ET BOUTEILLE DÉPOSÉES

Sauternes & Barsac

This small district encircled by the Graves produces only white wine, but this is white wine with a unique difference. The grapes are left on the vine long after the vintage and, when the conditions are ideal, a fungus will grow on the skins and dehydrate the grapes thus concentrating the sugar. The French call this the *pourriture noble*, or *nòble rot*. The shrivelled grapes with the concentrated sugary juice are then made into the rich dessert wine of Sauternes. The wine has an intensity of flavour and scent which has caused it to be described as a honey or nectar wine.

In 1855, a special classification was devised for Sauternes which placed Château d'Yquem in a class of its own – followed by eleven first growths and 12 seconds.

Unfortunately, Sauternes depends for its quality on ideal weather conditions and the ability of the grower to leave the grapes on the vine for as long as possible. Some of the smaller vineyards cannot afford to take the risk of bad weather in October and they pick much too early. Consequently, there is a world of difference between the great Châteaux and the lesser ones.

BORDEAUX BARGAINS

Fronsac, Bourg and Blaye

These three areas on the north east bank of the Dordogne are considered to produce wine of a lesser quality than the other claret making districts. In terms of greatness, this is probably fair but in considering everyday drinking they have certainly been underrated. Consequently, they can provide some genuine bargains.

Cerons

Wines from Cérons, Loupiac and Ste. Croix du Mont, close to the river Garonne and adjacent to Sauternes, are inclined to be rich and sweet but less expensive than their neighbours.

Entre-Deux-Mers

This vast area, lying between the two rivers is noted for its white, dryish wine. The quality is consistent, if not remarkable, and the wine is easily available at sensible prices.

The best wine from this area, however, comes from the strip of land which forms the east bank of the Garonne and is known as the Premiéres Côtes de Bordeaux. The wine here is red or white and is usually cheap and good value.

RECENT BORDEAUX VINTAGES

YEAR	COMMUNE	NOTES
1978	Medoc, Graves, Pomerol, St. Emilion	May be the best of the ten years 1967–78, but only time will tell.
1977	Medoc, Graves, Pomerol St. Emilion	Not good, but some will be suitable for early drinking.
1976	Medoc, Graves, Pomerol St. Emilion	Some wines very good, but a patchy vintage overall. Could be undervalued.
1975	Medoc, Graves, St. Emilion	Excellent, slow-maturing wines.
1975	Pomerol	Small but outstanding vintage; best wines fetching very high prices.
1974	Medoc, Graves, Pomerol St. Emilion	Disappointing – hopes held for some wines may never be realised.
1973	Medoc, Graves	Light, pleasant wines – not long-lived.
1973	Pomerol, St. Emilion	Fruity, but not tannic – drinking well now.
1972	Medoc, Graves, Pomerol, St. Emilion	Few good wines.
1971	Medoc, Graves	Some good wines, but a patchy overrated vintage.
1971	Pomerol, St. Emilion	Rather better, but a small crop.
1970	Medoc, Graves, Pomerol, St. Emilion	Very fine vintage; big crop and very consistent – still needs time.

Earlier worthwhile vintages: 1961, 1964, 1966

BEST RECENT YEARS FOR SWEET WHITE WINES

YEAR	COMMUNE	NOTES
1976	Sauternes, Barsac	Superb wines, but still good value
1975	Sauternes, Barsac	Very fine vintage, great depth and richness
1971	Sauternes, Barsac	Delicacy and richness; long-lived wines
1970	Sauternes, Barsac	Big, very good vintage – getting pricy

Burgundy

The old province of Bourgogne, Burgundy to the English, contains six quite distinct wine growing districts. In the north west, Chablis is detached from the rest of the Burgundian vineyards by some eighty or ninety kilometres. The Côte de Nuits and the Côte de Beaune form one continuous belt from Dijon to Chagny; then comes the Chalonnaise, small and fragmented, followed by the largest districts – Maconnais and Beaujolais. Some of the greatest names in wine lie just to the west of the N6 between Macon and Lyon.

Map of Burgundy
Some of the world's greatest wines come from the region shown here. The main area of production is the valley of the river Saône, between Tournus and Villefranche. But the finest wines are grown on the Côte d'Or, which stretches from Chagny to Dijon – a little to the north west of the Saône. Chablis, shown in the inset, is some 50 miles (80km) north west of Beaune. There is no significant wine production between the two districts. Chablis is exclusively devoted to white wine making, but throughout the rest of Burgundy white and red wine areas frequently overlap.

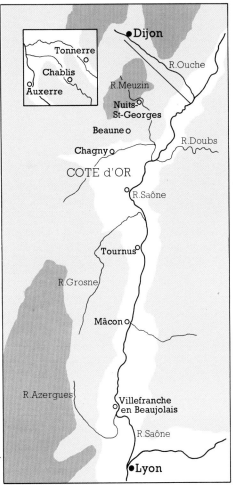

CONFUSION OF NAMES

The naming of wines in Burgundy, however, has always been a problem – and a problem which ensures that, even now, few people know exactly what they are getting when they buy, say, a Chassagne-Montrachet or a Gevrey-Chambertin. The cause is twofold. On the one hand, Burgundy is a region of small farmers and few big estates. The Napoleonic laws of inheritance have produced a situation in which many farmers may own vines in one vineyard – the Clos de Vougeot has 60 owners in 124 acres – so that buying a wine from a specified vineyard does not mean the same thing as buying a château-bottled Bordeaux wine.

On the other hand, the problem is confounded by twentieth-century laws governing the naming of wines. In the old days, wine was sold under the name of its vineyard, village or place of sale – depending on which was most appropriate or best known. The new laws required that wine be offered for sale only under the name of the place in which it was grown. The net result was that some excellent wines suddenly appeared under obscure names and some very respected names were left with only poorer quality wines.

Quality control

In the years that followed, many villages sought to remove the difficulty by annexing the name of their best vineyard. Consequently, the village of Gevrey became Gevrey-Chambertin, Chassagne became Chassagne-Montrachet, Nuits became Nuits-St. Georges. Unfortunately, this association with great names, though it has undoubtedly sold a lot of wine, does not confer the qualities of greatness upon the contents of the bottle.

Because of all these difficulties, and particularly the disparity of wines coming from different growers in the same vineyard, merchants have had to resort to blending to produce a consistent, recognisable wine.

The Appellations Contrôlée of Burgundy ensure that the quality of blended wines is maintained at a high standard, but the system of classification within each appellation (there are more than 100 of them) is unofficial.

To distinguish between fine wines and average quality wines would be simple enough if one had merely to know the names of the individual vineyards. Unfortunately, the labels of Burgundian bottles are sometimes less than helpful and it is a considerable advantage, in the search for fine wines, to know the names of the growers.

In all of this complexity it would be very easy to lose sight of the fact that Burgundy is one of the very greatest wine producing regions of the world. Its output is quite small – less than half that of Bordeaux – and its fine wines begin to have a rarity value the moment they are put in bottle. Even so, a very high percentage of what is produced is of excellent quality and of quite unique character. Many experienced wine drinkers will not shift from the view that the white Burgundies, perfect with food, are the finest of all dry white wines. Whilst the reds have a smoothly unfolding character of body and balance. A mature red burgundy from one of the better vineyards has a perfect poise – as if all the elements which make up the wine are being held together in the ideal balance with absolute ease. Drinking one can be a stunning experience. Wine lovers will debate for ever the relative merits of Burgundy and Bordeaux, in order to determine the world's finest red wine, but there is no method by which they can be placed in order of quality. Just enjoy them for the different pleasures they give.

TASTING WINE

The first step in assessing a wine is to take a good look at it. Seen against a well-lit white background, wine will soon reveal its clarity or otherwise and yield vital information about its age. Stage two is to smell the wine. The smell is important in establishing the condition of the wine. After swirling the wine in the glass, the experienced taster will rely on his nose to tell him whether he should actually taste the wine. A good smell should be confirmed by the taste – examined by swirling the wine around the tongue and giving it time to make its impressions, which may be numerous. Finally, the wine is discarded by spitting. Professional tasters may have to assess 20 wines in one session, so any attempt to swallow the wine would certainly affect their judgement before the end.

Classification

There are four ranks in the Burgundian system of classification. The first and highest, is *Grand Cru* (sometimes called *tête de cuvée*) and is applied only to the best vineyard of each village. The label of such wine will carry the vineyard name; e.g., Montrachet – but will not show the name of the village or commune. Since the title *Grand Cru* is applied to the vineyard and not to the vintage, it is not certain to appear on the label; it is certainly not compulsory.

The next rank is *Premier Cru*, or first growths. These wines will show first the name of their commune, e.g. Chassagne-Montrachet, followed by the name of its vineyard, e.g. Cailleret. It may be a blend of several *Premier Cru* vineyards, in which case the label must include the words *Premier Cru* after the commune name.

The third rank is officially classified as *Appellation Communale* and sometimes called second growths; in practice, neither is likely to show on the label.

The fourth rank is not allowed to call its wine anything other than Bourgogne, although it may well be that it comes from within some very good communes.

BURGUNDIAN PRECEDENCE

These labels illustrate the difficulty of determining the true status of the wine. The red Corton, from the vineyard Clos du Roi, is one of the finest of *Grand Cru* Burgundies, but the label gives little indication of its quality. On the other hand, the Clos des Lambrays, although a very fine wine, is a *Premier Cru* – not a Grand Cru as claimed by the label. The wines from the Hospice de Beaune and the vineyard of Grèves are both Premier Cru, but the fact is not stated. The Macon Villages is an example of the third level of Burgundy. 'Villages' indicates that it is made from the produce of selected communes within the district. The reference to the Domaine de Montbellet does not indicate that the wine comes from a single vineyard.

Chablis

Chablis is the most northerly of Burgundies and is the only district devoted entirely to the production of white wine.

The wine, especially when young, is very dry, rather hard and slightly green. There is very little top rank Chablis, though what there is can, in a good year, be remarkable. Chablis is very long lived and in time will begin to take on a golden hue mixed with the green. In its maturity the hardness and cutting quality of its taste becomes less earthy and more ethereal. Perhaps it is a difficult taste to acquire. Unfortunately, most Chablis sold in most wine stores do very little justice to the name and you should be very careful in making a selection. Without close reading of the label you could easily be buying something which is not Chablis at all.

To be sure of quality, look for a good year and the words *Grand Cru* or *Premier Cru* (not forgetting *Appellation Contrôllée* – essential for all Burgundies). Wine labelled, simply, Chablis or Petit Chablis may come from well outside the area which grows fine wine and, especially in a poor year, is capable of being a major disappointment – yet it is unlikely to be cheap.

BURGUNDY AND FOOD

The association of Burgundy, as a geographical entity, as much with food as with wine is entirely natural and inescapable. From this ancient province comes much of the best poultry, game, beef and dairy produce in France. The restaurants of such towns as Dijon, Villefranche and Lyon have international reputations for their cooking of regional food. The range of wines produced, from Chablis in the north to Beaujolais in the South, are sufficient to provide for any course at any meal. Traditionally, the white Burgundies are the ideal companions of fish dishes. This is particularly true of Chablis and Pouilly-Fuissé, but the great white wines of Burgundy if you are lucky enough to get hold of them, are best consumed without the accompaniment of food. The same is true of the finest red Burgundies, though there should be no objection to drinking a Premier Cru Beaune, Fixin, Chambolle-Musigny or Gevrey-Chambertin with the very best red meat or game. In general, though, it is more sensible to look for the less expensive wines from the Chalonnais and the Maconnais for wines to drink with everyday meals.

The Côte d'Or

The Cote d'Or consists of the Côte de Nuits and the Côte de Beaune, and it produces red and white wine. The rolling hills above the river Saône are drenched in the names of wines so famous that it is hard to believe they can be so close together – like having eleven of the world's finest soccer players in the same team. Santenay, Chassagne-Montrachet, Puligny-Montrachet, Meursault, Volnay, Pommard, Beaune, Aloxe-Corton, Nuits-St. Georges, Vougeot, Chambolle-Musigny, Gevrey-Chambertin, Fixin and so it goes on. Whether from communes or specific vineyards the wines comes in endless variety of character – and all of it unmistakably from the very heart of France.

1972 1972

Aloxe-Corton
1er Cru
Mise du Domaine - Appellation Contrôlée

Prince de Merode
Serrigny. (Côte-d'Or).

Red wines

Although good red wine comes from Santenay, Volnay and Pommard, the best comes from the Côte de Nuits. Here, the wines are deeper in colour, bigger bodied, rich and much in demand. The most expensive wines come from the vineyards around the village of Vosne-Romanée, where even the second rank wines are superb.

The wines from the district of Nuits-St. Georges have all the characteristics of red Burgundies without being so striking as the Romanées. The name has been popular in America and Britain for many years but there are doubts as to how much of it has been genuine.

Chambertin is the other great name from this district – and another which has been subjected to great abuse. Many people believe that Chambertin and its neighbouring *Grand Cru* of Clos de Bèze are the finest of all Burgundies, even the finest of all red wines – they may be right. Certainly the wines themselves, strong, well-rounded and long-lived, have enough confidence to stake their claims.

Morey St. Denis and Fixin both make wines of quality, and Chambolle-Musigny is another in the big league.

White wines

Most of the white wines of the Côte d'Or, and certainly the best, come from the Côte de Beaune. Here we find the names that are synonymous with Everest in the world of wine: Corton-Charlemagne, Meursault and Montrachet.

Do not be confused by the name Corton-Charlemagne: it is not the village wine borrowing the name of its best vineyard. Corton-Charlemagne is the vineyard, and one of the greatest in the world, the village is Aloxe-Corton – a name you are far more likely to meet in your wine store.

The distinctive character of Corton-Charlemagne is its fullness of flavour – a rare, powerful spicy taste, a sweeping pervasive flavour which, once tasted, is never forgotten.

The other wines from this district, though they cannot compare in greatness are still very good.

Meursault is likely to provide the best value on the Côte de Beaune. It produces eminently consistent wine at all levels and is not hard to find. The neighbouring villages of Chassagne-Montrachet and Puligny-Montrachet produce, from their five *Grand Cru* vineyards, some of the most beautiful of all dry white wines. The *Grand Cru* wines are prohibitively expensive and all the named vineyards are very much in demand. Nevertheless, the simple village wine is very often way above other third and fourth rank wines and should never be ignored.

BUYING BURGUNDY

Since the great Burgundy scandals of some years ago, which produced a welcome tightening of Appellation Contrôlée regulations, the reputation and price of wines from the region has soared to unimaginable levels. It is hardly possible, now, to recommend fine Burgundies to a wine drinker of modest means. There are some useful tips to follow, however: white Burgundies, though not cheap, cost significantly less than comparable red wines and it is possible to acquire some of the greatest names without breaking the bank. Lesser red wines can be overpriced, and one must return to the habitual comment about all Burgundies – *look for wines from reputable growers*.

Mâconnais & Chalonnais

The Maconnais is responsible for a great deal of sound, reliable, but unremarkable white wine. It does, however, harbour the apellation of Pouilly-Fuissé – another of the most famous names in wine. Pouilly-Fuissé is a more subtle wine than those of the Côte d'Or, but has all the hallmarks of good Burgundy. Other good wines from the area come from St. Veran – a name which is cropping up more and more now that alternative value is so important – and Pouilly-Vinzelles.

The Chalonnais is a very small district producing good, consistent wine, both red and white. The best red comes from Mercurey and the white from Montagny. The Chalonnais is another area to remember in the search for good value, but neither Côte Chalonnaise nor Chalon-sur-Saône is certain to appear on the label. Look for the wines already mentioned, or Rully and Givry as alternatives.

Beaujolais

The modern requirement among wine drinkers is immediacy – instant consumption of wine that is ready to drink. Few people are prepared to keep wine for any length of time even though it increases in price at a rate which at least keeps pace with inflation. Beaujolais is the perfect answer – the epitomy of young, grapy, red wine.

The Beaujolais is distinguished from the rest of Burgundy by a number of features. Firstly, it produces as much wine as the rest of Burgundy put together. Secondly, the land is much higher than the Côte d'Or, the climate a degree more southern and, thirdly, the grape is the Gamay, which has almost disappeared from the rest of Burgundy but thrives here on the granite soil.

The system of classification in Beaujolais is simpler and less sophisticated than elsewhere. There are rather more than sixty villages in the area; to be able to call their wine Beaujolais they have only to ensure it reaches 9% alcohol, 10% will entitle it to the qualification *Supérieur*. The growers in Beaujolais are much given to the use of sugar in the fermentation process, so the required levels of alcohol are not hard to achieve.

In the northern part of the district, thirty-five villages whose wine is considered to be rather more distinctive in its regional character are designated Beaujolais-Villages. These are the second rank growths in comparative terms, although there are no official first and second growths in Beaujolais.

The top rank is occupied by nine villages which have their own appelations and are the *Grand Cru*: Juliénas, St. Amour, Moulin-à-Vent, Chénas, Fleurie, Chiroubles, Morgon, Brouilly and Côte-de-Brouilly. These wines have more body and keeping qualities than the rest of Beaujolais. The smooth, sweetish, grapy flavour takes on a new dimension after some months in bottle.

There is now a considerable fashion for drinking Beaujolais *en primeur* – the first produced wine of the vintage. The law permits the selling of this wine from the 15th November of each year. There is usually a frantic rush to transport the new wine to all parts of the World, but apart from commercial considerations, it can hardly be worth the effort. Even the humbler and shorter-lived Beaujolais is better a month or two later.

BURGUNDY VINTAGES

RED WINES: CÔTE d'OR

1978	Likely to be a great vintage
1977	No better than average, some very slight wines
1976	Magnificent; wines for keeping
1975	Very small, unsatisfactory crop
1974	Below average, but big crop
1973	Fairly good vintage, but not for keeping
1972	A good year, just about ready for drinking
1971	A great year, but a small crop
1970	A very good year; drink now

WHITE WINES: CÔTE d'OR AND CHABLIS

1978	Great wine anticipated
1977	Patchy: some good wines, some below average
1976	Superb wines everywhere
1975	Excellent; drinking well now
1974	Good to very good; drink now
1973	Pleasant wines, good character
1972	Some very good; Chablis poor
1971	Great wines, aging well
1970	Big vintage, good all-round wines

BEAUJOLAIS

1978	Big vintage, excellent wines
1977	Only average
1976	One of the very best years

The Loire Valley

The wine growing sections of the Loire valley straggle from the Atlantic coast near Nantes for almost 600 miles eastwards to the town of Pouilly-sur-Loire – only eighty miles from the Côte d'Or The character of Loire wines, therefore, varies considerably. At the mouth of the river, Muscadet has established itself as one of the important white wines of France. It is light, dry but quite gentle, and excellent with fish. Several hundred miles nearer the source, the wines of Pouilly and Sancerre are of that character known as flinty. This description derives from the smell which the Sauvignon grape imparts to the wine – a whiff of gun-flint. Pouilly-Fumé (not to be confused with Pouilly-Fuissé) is the best of such wines. Pouilly-sur-Loire is made from the Chasselas grape.

Anjou and Touraine

The central Loire produces wine which, at its best is sweet – not full and overpoweringly rich, but with a delicate fruitiness and a touch of sharpness. This is Anjou, best known outside France for its delicately perfumed, sweetish Rosé. But Anjou is also the home of some excellent white wines. The best of them come from Savennières in the Coteaux de la Loire; they are increasing in price all the time but a true appreciation of French wine is impossible without trying them.

Quarts de Chaume is probably the sweetest wine of the region, and Bonnézeaux the most surprising, but all are worth getting to know.

The wines from the Coteaux du Layon are relatively cheap, light, fruity and very refreshing.

The red wine of the Loire comes from Chinon, Bourgueil and St. Nicholas de Bourgueil. The wine is very light, fresh and may be cooled to good effect.

The last important area of the Loire is Vouvray. The wine may be dry, semi-sweet, sweet, *pétillant* or sparkling. The best of Vouvray will be light but full, remarkable in strength and surprisingly long lasting.

Alsace

This curious region, tucked away under the Vosges mountains, on the French side of the Rhine but on the German side of the mountains, produces excellent wine – usually at excellent prices.

Unlike most French wines they are named after the grape variety and not the places in which they are grown. The grapes, not surprisingly, are mostly Germanic varieties: Riesling, Sylvaner and Gewürztraminer. The Muscat, Pinot Blanc and the Pinot Gris (known locally as Tokay d'Alsace) are all used to a lesser extent.

The wines are not really like German wines, being much drier and somewhat stronger, but they are quite unlike the rest of French wines. Alsace seldom produces great vintages, and there have been many disappointments in recent years, but the spicy flavour and the uncomplicated nature of the wine makes it an excellent accompaniment to the typically rich Alsatian food.

When buying Alsace wines it is useful to remember the names of some of the shippers: wines from Hugel, Trimbach, Dopff & Irion, Preiss Zimmer, Schlumberger and Josemeyer are widely available and carry a good reputation.

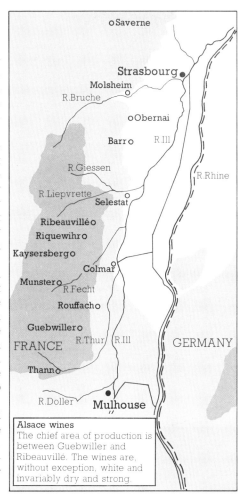

Alsace wines
The chief area of production is between Guebwiller and Ribeauvillé. The wines are, without exception, white and invariably dry and strong.

The Rhône Valley

The part of the Rhône valley which is responsible for the production of over 300 million litres of wine annually, stretches from Lyons in the north to Avignon in the south. Between Valence and Bollene there is virtually no wine growing – so the northern districts of Côte Rôtie, Condrieu and Hermitage are cut off from the southern areas of Châteauneuf-du-Pape, Lirac, Tavel, Rasteau, and Beaumes-de-Venise by some fifty miles. Within that distance there is a significant change of climate. The north has a typical continental climate, with warm summers and mild winters, but the south is almost Mediterranean, with very hot and dry summers and somewhat erratic rainfall. The entire valley, however, is subject to the ravages of the Mistral which can blow from the north throughout the year.

Unusually for France, the wines of this region are unlikely to be the produce of a single grape variety. Indeed, some wines may use as many as 13 different grapes. In the northern districts, the Syrah is the most important grape; in the south Grenache predominates. In this southern climate, wines of great strength and longevity are made. They are the 'biggest' wines in France

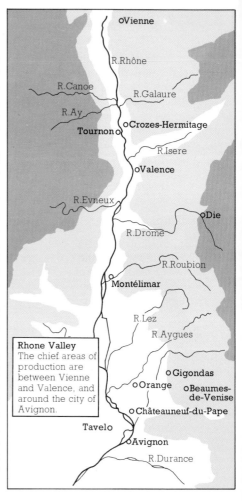

Rhone Valley
The chief areas of production are between Vienne and Valence, and around the city of Avignon.

Rhône-White

White wines from the Rhône are not very well known and there are not many of them, but they maintain excellent quality and display unusual characteristics. On the whole, they are more golden than other, more northern, white wines. They are dry but full-flavoured, pungent but deliciously scented. Even a humble example conveys an impression of 'bigness'. One only wishes that they were more easily obtainable.

The most famous of these white wines is Château Grillet. Unfortunately, most people will never have the opportunity to try it because it is one of the world's rarities – having a production of less than a thousand bottles in some years.

Condrieu produces wine of a similar kind, but it, too, is rare and seldom exported. Hermitage and Crozes-Hermitage, though better known for their red wines, both produce very fine white – but, again, it can be hard to find.

Probably the most unusual wine in the whole region comes from Beaumes-de-Venise. This is a sweet muscat wine, slightly fortified, and having the qualities of freshness and lightness which normally belong to wines which are much less sweet.

Rhône-Red

Unlike the white wines, the reds of the Rhône valley include some names which are household words: Hermitage and Châteauneuf-du-Pape being the most famous. But, although these wines have justly earned their fame, they have seldom been used to their best advantage. Hermitage, particularly, suffers in this respect. In a world dedicated to the immediate consumption of wine, Hermitage is almost an anachronism. It is very slow maturing and may not reveal its true nature for ten or fifteen years. Because of this, it can be bought as a young wine for very reasonable prices and, when mature, will be worth a great deal. It is unlikely, however, that any serious wine drinker would want to sell his carefully nurtured Hermitage.

Crozes-Hermitage is an only slightly inferior alternative to the great name, but somewhat cheaper and fairly easily available.

The description Côte du Rhône is much used for the cheaper wines of the region but it is exceptionally vague for an appellation contrôlée. Better to look for Côtes-du-Rhône Villages which ensures that the wine is from the top 10% of communes.

TAVEL ROSÉ

The Rhône valley is the home of a truly excellent pink wine. Tavel is a dark, orange-brown rosé, more positive in flavour than those of Anjou or the Jura, and giving an impression of stature that few rosés achieve.

Although Tavel is sold young, like all pink wines, it is considered by some experienced drinkers to need up to ten years in bottle. It will, however, provide excellent wine after only three years – at which stage of its life it is not expensive.

Chef de Rosé
Tavel is a near neighbour of Chateauneuf-du-Pape, and has similar qualities of strength and long life. It is an excellent companion to provencal food.

Châteauneuf-du-Pape

The southernmost giant name in French viticulture is Châteauneuf-du-Pape. Situated between Avignon and Orange, the vineyards of Châteauneuf are remarkable for their apparent absence of soil. The vines appear to be growing in the midst of millions of round stones – not a trace of soil can be seen. These stones, however, protect the moisture in the soil during dry years and act as night storage heaters, ensuring long and consistent warmth for the vines. The wine here is the strongest of any in France – it can reach 15% alcohol – and it is strong in body and flavour also. Some of the best estates, which may be called *châteaux* or *Domaines*, produce a very dark, slow-maturing wine. Some of the lesser vineyards make a quick maturing wine which is ready to drink in one or two years – but it is not comparable with the bigger, older wines. Much of the younger wine comes from the neighbouring area of Gigondas.

Although similar in basic character to Châteauneuf, these wines offer excellent value for money and, though they will repay keeping for three or four years, they are suitable for drinking earlier.

Champagne

The vineyards of Champagne are the most northerly in France. They begin some 85km (50 miles) east of Paris and continue for a similar distance north east to Rheims. This is gently rolling country with a very deep chalk soil. Both the Pinot Noir and Chardonnay grapes grow well there and most Champagne is made from a combination of both.

The chief characteristic of Champagne, fizziness in the bottle, came about as a result of the geography and climate of the vineyards. Originally, Champagne was made like any other wine, but because of the northern climate, fermentation was temporarily curtailed by the onset of winter. In Spring, when warmer weather arrived, fermentation would begin again. It was the cellar-master of the Abbey of Hautvillers, a certain Dom Pérignon, who discovered the merits of bottling the wine durings its secondary fermentation. This, fundamentally, is the system by which Champagne is made today. It is a more complicated and labour-intensive method than for other wines; Champagne is, therefore, necessarily more expensive than most others.

CHAMPAGNE PRESENTATION

Vintage wines are not made every year, but only when the grape harvest has special qualities to recommend it.

NAME OF BOTTLE		CONTENTS
A	Quarter bottle	6½ fluid oz. (18 cl)
B	Half bottle	13 fluid oz. (36cl)
C	Imperial pint	19½ fluid oz. (54cl)
D ☆	Bottle	26 fluid oz. (73cl)
E ☆	Magnum	2 bottles
F	Jeroboam	4 bottles
G	Rehoboam	6 bottles
H	Methuselah	8 bottles
✪	Salmanazar	10½ bottles
✪	Balthazar	16 bottles
✪	Nebuchadnezzar	20 bottles

☆Champagne is at its best in bottles and magnums

✪No longer sold commercially

HOW CHAMPAGNE IS MADE

The Champagne method

There are four critical operations in the making of Champagne. The first is blending. Every Champagne is a blend, the object being to marry the best and most suitable characteristics of different vineyards, from different parts of the region. Around Rheims and in the valley of the Maîne grow the black grapes. The white grapes come from the south-western part of the region, near Epernay. Most Champagnes are a blend of grapes from each district. The exception is Blanc de Blanc, a wine which is made from white grapes only.

Remuage

While the wine is undergoing its secondary fermentation in the bottle a deposit of dead yeast cells is gradually formed. This has to be removed from the bottle without losing the essential bubbles. The method for doing this is to encourage the deposit to attach itself to the cork so that it can be lifted out in one simple operation. To achieve this, the bottles are stacked at an angle, cork downwards. Then they are turned and gently shaken each day, until the sediment is all on the cork.

Degorgement

When the wine has finished its period of maturation a man called the *degorgeur* removes the cork and about 5cm (2ins.) of wine. The bottle is then topped up with a mixture of sugar and wine and receives its final cork. Sometimes the first cork is removed after the neck of the bottle has been frozen so that a frozen plug of wine is taken out with it – thus regulating the amount of wine which is lost from the bottle.

The topping up process is critical to the style of the wine, especially the sweeter varieties. When the wine has reached the end of its secondary fermentation it has used up all of its natural sugar. In practice, even the driest wines are slightly sweetened.

The process of remuage.

Other French wines

The wines of the remaining areas of France, chiefly Provence, the Jura, Languedoc and Roussillon, are mostly vin ordinaire and VDQS. But, as always, there are pockets of quality. The best wines of Provence are strong and pink, that from Cassis being the most notable.

The wines of The Jura and Savoie are seldom seen outside France but visitors will find them charming and unusual. The most respected wine of the Jura is called *vin jaune* (yellow wine) and is very long-lived. The best of these is Château Châlon, a wine which is left open to the air for several years after fermentation. A yeasty crust forms on the surface and the slow oxygenation gradually produces a deep yellow colour in the wine.

The white wines of Savoie are completely colourless with a gentle, clear and soft flavour. The best wines come from Crépy and Seyssel, the latter having a particularly good sparkling version.

The wines of Languedoc and Roussillon are, with very few exceptions, rather dull and not worth seeking out. the white wine of Clairette-du-Languedoc and the red of Fitou deserve more attention than the rest.

PROVINCIAL BARGAINS

Traditionally, the Mediterranean wine growing areas have been the source of much cheap wine, often used by shippers as the basis for their own blended products – usually sold under brand names. With the growth of the VDQS system of control things began to change, and many wines of quite distinct regional character began to emerge. Now, much of the wine from Provence is sold as VDQS and a fair proportion has been elevated to the status of Appellation Contrôlée. White wines tend to be strong and very dry; reds rather bland and unsubtle. Nevertleless, these wines represent good value for everyday drinking. The Costières du Gard, at the southern extremity of the Rhône valley, is a VDQS district with a better reputation than most.

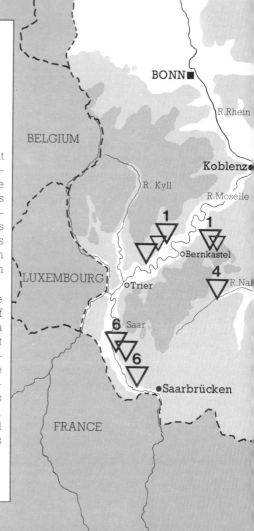

GERMANY

Although the German vineyards are at the northern limit of successful viticulture, wine has been produced there since Roman times. When the Romans departed, the monasteries and commercial winemakers of Charlemagne's Holy Roman Empire made tremendous developments in both the production and trading of wine. Their influence can still be seen today.

Trier was the second city of the Roman empire and has been the seat of Archbishops since. Its importance as a centre of one of the world's greatest wine growing regions is not coincidental. The church in Germany was the original source of control and influence. Some of the earliest wine laws can be traced to church involvement, and many of the monastic names still adorn the labels of some of Germany's most notable wines.

Key

	Sea level – 600 ft (180 m)
	600–3000 ft (180–900 m)
	Above 3000 ft (900 m)
	Oceans/sea
	Other territories
▽	White wine production
▼	Red wine production
■	Principal/Capital Cities
●	Main Towns
○	Small Towns
---	International Frontiers
∿	Rivers

Principle wine regions

This deals with the regions whose wines are best known outside Germany. Wine is also produced in the south east of the country, in the vicinity of Baden and Württemberg, but these wines, though good, are not exported in quantity.

1	Moselle
2	Rheingau
3	Franconia
4	Nahe
5	Rheinhessen
6	Saar-Ruwer
7	Rheinpfalz

Scale 0   20   40 km.

D.D.R.

2 Wiesbaden   Frankfurt
                        ●Offenbach
Mainz●
Darmstadt   **3**
5   Würzburg
R.Rhein   **3**
        R.Main
Worms○
Ludwigshafen●
  ●Mannheim
7   R.Neckar

●Karlsruhe

●Stuttgart

GERMAN WINE LAW

As we saw on page 24, German wines are controlled in three groups: *Deutscher Tafelwein, Qualitätswein*, which is the basic level of quality status, and *Qualitätswein mit Prädikat*, meaning wines with special attributes. The words used to describe these attributes are: **Kabinet; Spätlese,** both made from late gathered grapes; **Auslese**, late gathered but in selected bunches; **Beerenauslese**, individually picked grapes which have been attacked by the *'noble rot'* (called *edel faule* by the Germans) and similar to the fungus that grows on the Sauternes grapes; **Trokenbeerenauslese**, using the same method as the Beerenauslese but using the really shrivelled, almost dried grapes. There is also an *Eiswein* made from grapes picked during the winter whilst they are frozen. Most of the higher categories of Pradikätwein are rather exotic and expensive.

These styles are maintained by a very precise system of control which includes a chemical analysis and the passing of a tasting test by a panel of experts who judge the wines on a Points system.

Sweetening

Unfortunately for most wine drinkers, the German quality control system is bound up with a good deal of science and technology, as well as law. To achieve an understanding of this it is important to remember that the German climate is somewhat harsh and unpredictable for viticulture to be at its best, but, in spite of this, the very best wines are sweet. Sweet wines demand that the grapes be left on the vines until as late as possible. This is only possible during prolonged fine autumn weather, which does not occur every year in Germany. Without the right weather conditions entirely natural wines will not be sweet, and in a very bad year they will be undrinkable.

German wine makers strive to achieve the ideal balance between sugar and acidity. This results in a wine which has approximately nine degrees of alcohol and a trace of residual sugar to provide the balance. In most years this can only be done by adding sugar. In Germany, such a practice is not only permitted – it is standard and necessary. The method used to be to add sugar and water, stopping the fermentation with sulphur before the sugar completely disappeared.

The modern method is to ferment the wine to the very end of the sugar content and then add sweetening in the form of unfermented grape juice. The grape juice is prevented from fermenting by a very fine filtration process which removes the yeasts before they can do their work. The filtration process was originally developed as a means of eliminating the use of sulphur as a stopper. This use of grape juice, or *süss-reserve* is much criticised by purists, but the Germans claim that, given time, a wine made in this way will settle down to a satisfactory balance of sugar and alcohol – losing the initial predominating sweetness.

All of this laboratory work, however, does not mean that the German wine maker has resorted to short cuts. German growers are as concerned as they ever were to produce the very best wine. It is the vicissitudes of the weather and the palate of the consumer which enforce the necessity of blending and sweetening. Not unnaturally, the German winemakers have made an art of the technology which they must incorporate in their skills and nobody should doubt the integrity of Qualitätswein or Pradikätswein.

UNDERSTANDING LABELS

Single and collective vineyards
The top label is from a single vineyard (*Einzellage*), in this case **Hassel**. The bottom label represents a collective site (*Grosslage*) – this one is **Michelsberg**. An Einzellage will always be preceded by the parish – **Hattenheim**; a Grosslage by the district (*Bereich*) – **Piesporter**. Usually, but not necessarily, the Prädikat wines (QmP) come from Einzellagen, the ordinary qualitätswein (QbA) from Grosslagen.

65

THE PRINCIPLE WINE REGIONS OF GERMANY

REGION	TYPES OF WINE	COMMENTS
MOSELLE (Inc. Saar-Ruwer)	White: sweet, semi-sweet	The most delicate and fragrant wines in Germany; light, fresh and uplifting – in great years they have layer upon layer of subtle flavours; best wines from the middle-Moselle. *Value tip: wines from Brauneberg Zeltingen, Graach and Wehlen. Saar wines in good years.*
RHEINGAU	White: sweet, semi-sweet	Excellent, and many great, wines of tremendous variety; some spicy and pungent, others gentle and fragrant. *Value tip: wines from Mittelheim, Hattenheim and Geisenheim.*
NAHE	White: sweet, semi-sweet	Fine, delicate wines with pronounced grapiness and scent. *Value tip: wines from Niederhausen*
RHEINHESSEN	White: sweet, semi-sweet	The source of the world famous Liebfraumlich – made from Sylvaner and Müller-Thurgau grapes. The only wines of outstanding quality come from Nierstein and Oppenheim. *Value tip: wines from Nackenheim.*
RHEINPFALZ (The Palatinate)	White: sweet, some red	Fuller-flavoured wines than many others in Germany, more robust but lacking the scent and freshness of Moselles and Rheingaus. Many new grape varieties are used here. *Value tip: wines from the einzellagen of Wachenheim and Bad Dürkheim.*
FRANCONIA	White: dry, sweet	Excellent wines to accompany meals of typical German food; dry wines are usually called *Steinwein*; best wines come from Würzburg, Randersaker and Iphofen. *Value tip: late-gathered Steinwein*

The Moselle

Moselle wines of quality come from the Middle Moselle – a relatively short stretch of river but banks are dense with vines. The grey slate soil imparts a cutting edge to the powerfully scented wine, but it remains gentle and easy to drink. This district contains the justly famous names of Piesport and Bernkastel. Both towns export some of the world's finest wines but you must be careful to distinguish between individual vineyards and *grosslage*. The *grosslagen* of Michelsberg (Piesport) and Kurfurstlay (Bernkastel) total some eight thousand acres. The wine is good but nowhere near the same class as the *einzellagen* of Goldtropfchen and Doktor. Doktor, which rises almost out of the streets of the picture-book town of Bernkastel, was once one of Germany's most expensive wines, but the wine is not sweet enough for today's taste. Nevertheless, it is still an experience to be recommended.

The Saar and the Ruwer, both of which flow into the Moselle near the border with Luxembourg, produce very fine, delicate wines. Without a hot summer, however, they are almost unable to produce anything of consequence and a bad summer would result in next to nothing.

Scenic vineyards
The impressive scenery of the Middle-Moselle is much used by growers of the region to decorate their labels.

The Rheingau

The Rheingau consists of the foothills of the Taunus mountains where they slope down to the Rhine. The wine here, at its best, has the flowery scent of the riesling but has more 'golden' depth than Moselle. Some of the finest wines come from Johannisberg (which also serves as the Bereich name for the area), Rüdesheim, Hocheim, Rauenthal, Hattenheim, Hallgarten, and Erbach.

The Nahe

The river Nahe joins the Rhine near Bingen after flowing through gentle attractive countryside. Bad Kreuznach and Schlossböckelheim have the best vineyards but the district, as a whole, produces a high percentage of fine wine – despite its rather small total output. The wines are clean and fresh tasting, like Moselle, but having some of the deeper flavour of the Rheingau.

Romantic labels
New EEC laws have not inhibited German label designers, as the typically romantic Kiedrich label shows. The Kupfergrübe vineyard above, is one of the finest on the Nahe.

The Rheinhessen

The Rheinhessen is on the opposite side of the Rhine to the Rheingau. In terms of fine wine production it is the wrong side. Most of the wine grown here is destined to become Liebfraumilch – not that there is anything wrong with Liebfraumilch, but it is blended, sweetish, innocuous and far from the quality of the Rheingau wines. The best wines come from Nierstein and Oppenheim.

The Rheinpfalz

This district, under the lee of the Haardt mountains – the German continuation of the Vosges – has a warmer and sunnier climate than most other parts of Germany. A great variety of grapes are grown here and much of the wine is sweet and rather heady – the sweetest comes from Forst – but there are some beautifully balanced wines in and around Wachenheim.

Three of the principal vineyards of the Rheinhessen and Rheinpfalz (Palatinate)

There have been vineyards in Italy since before Roman times and until the establishment of vineyards in the Empire, the legions in the occupied territories were supplied with wine from Italy.

Today, Italy produces more wine than any other country in the world. Although the Italian wine farmers, who are great individualists, are mainly producing wine for local consumption, Italy has done much to improve the quality reputation of its wines in recent years.

Much of Italy is concerned with wine production, but its geography and climate ensure that the variety, both in kind and quality, is considerable. The north of Italy has a much cooler climate than the south, being influenced by the Alps rather than the Mediterranean. Much of the landscape is mountainous so that many of Italy's wines can be classified as hill wines.

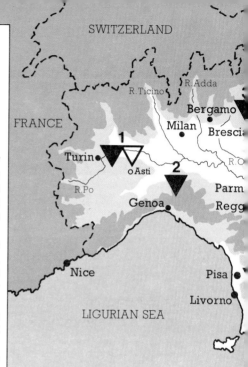

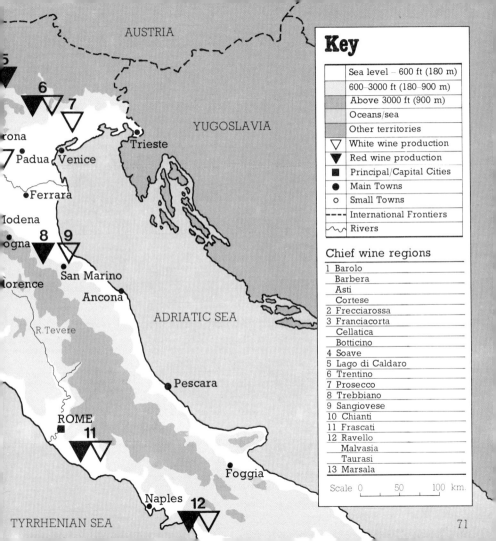

AUSTRIA

YUGOSLAVIA

Trieste

ona

7 Padua Venice

Ferrara

Iodena

ogna 8 9

San Marino

Iorence Ancona

ADRIATIC SEA

R.Tevere

Pescara

ROME 11

Foggia

Naples 12

TYRRHENIAN SEA

Key

	Sea level – 600 ft (180 m)
	600–3000 ft (180–900 m)
	Above 3000 ft (900 m)
	Oceans/sea
	Other territories
▽	White wine production
▼	Red wine production
■	Principal/Capital Cities
●	Main Towns
o	Small Towns
-----	International Frontiers
∼∿	Rivers

Chief wine regions

1	Barolo
	Barbera
	Asti
	Cortese
2	Frecciarossa
3	Franciacorta
	Cellatica
	Botticino
4	Soave
5	Lago di Caldaro
6	Trentino
7	Prosecco
8	Trebbiano
9	Sangiovese
10	Chianti
11	Frascati
12	Ravello
	Malvasia
	Taurasi
13	Marsala

Scale 0   50   100 km.

71

Nomenclature

In 1963, soon after the establishment of the EEC, the Italian Government issued a decree setting up a control system to give the country's fine wine quality status, and so fall into line with the systems well established in other wine producing countries like France and Germany. DOC or Denominazione d'Origine Controllata and DOCG or Denominazione d'Origine Controllata e Garantita are the titles given to wines with guaranteed names of origin. Some fifteen years after this initiation only about 10% of the total production had achieved this distinction. All classified wines will bear the DOC description on the label. Many Italian wines are described by the grape variety which will also be associated with its region of origin if it has quality status.

Unfortunately for those who are used only to the French or German systems, Italian wines, including some of the classified ones, may bear names which have nothing to do with grape or region, names which may be sheer romanticism. The DOC laws have not prevented this, neither should they, but they have ensured the addition of regional information to the labels of classified wines.

Italy's reputation as a wine growing country is based largely on its red wines, of which there is an astounding variety. Great and exceptional wines are produced much less frequently than in France, but they do occur – as do many wines which are consistently good.

As a wine exporter, Italy has established a reputation for large quantities of acceptable cheap wine. Under the present laws, the quality is steadily improving and the price is rising, but Italian wine looks like providing good value for money for many years to come.

BARDOLINO
DENOMINAZIONE DI ORIGINE CONTROLLATA
FINATELLO

VINO IMBOTTIGLIATO NELLA ZONA DI PRODUZIONE DA
EFFEPIVI · VERONA · ITALIA
FOR
FINDLATER MATTA AGENCIES LONDON W1
150 cl   PRODUCE OF ITALY   11 % VOL.

Northern Italy

In the north-west corner, between the Alps and the sea, is the region known as Piedmont – where some of Italy's finest wines are produced. The best known of these wines are Barolo and Barbaresco. Barolo wines are exceptionally dark, strong and long-lived, with a powerful scent and a big flavour of fruit. Barbaresco is very similar but not quite so mouth-filling and expensive.

Piedmont is also responsible for the production of Asti Spumante, the town of Asti being right in the centre of the region. This wine, which is made from the Moscato grape is rich, sweet and sparkling and has nothing in common with Champagne.

North-East Italy

In this corner of Italy, the finest wines will be found in the vicinity of Verona. Valpolicella, Bardolino and Soave are famous names all over the wine drinking world – and not just because quantities are exported. Valpolicella and Bardolino are the opposite in the red wine scale to Barolo and Barbaresco. They are light, pale (Bardolino is almost a rosé) and must be drunk when they are very young to be tasted at their best. They are very easy drinking and have readily established a market outside Italy. Soave is considered to be Italy's best white wine. It is very uncomplicated, light dry and straightforward and, like the red wines of Verona, should be drunk young.

To the north of Verona are the wine growing area of Trentino and Alto Adige. Here, near the Tyrol, many of the grapes are German and the white wines are Germanic in character. One of the best of them is Terlaner Edel Muskateller, which is a rich sweet dessert wine. The gentle red wines from this district are not easily available outside Italy. Lago di Caldaro may, however, be found in reasonable quantities. In Germany and Austria it is known as Kalterersee.

Central Italy

In the valley of the River Po, little wine is grown because of frequent flooding. But a little to the south of the river, on the way to Modena is the home of one of Europe's most unusual wines, Lambrusco. This wine is sparkling, sweet and red, characteristics which, rather surprisingly are causing it to find favour outside Italy. There are indications, though, that the exported version may not be entirely natural. The real thing is said not to travel and so one must suspect the addition of chemicals to exported bottles.

Further south, in the area between Florence and Siena, Italy's best known wine is made. This is the ever popular Chianti – familiar to the world in its flask-shaped bottle with a straw case (a bottle which is rapidly disappearing).

Chianti is probably the most variable wine in the world; few wines with a respected regional name have such a disparity between their best and worst versions. Much of the dreadful stuff which used to appear under the name of Chianti has vanished with the new wine laws, but the ordinary wine produced by the small farmers can be decidedly rough. The best wines, on the other hand, are grown and made with as much care as any in France or Germany.

Chianti is made from four kinds of grapes, which all ferment together. When the fermentation is beginning to slow down an unfermented must of the same blend of grapes is added. The fermentation picks up again as a result of this process – known as '*il governo*' – and ensures that there is just a touch of fermentation in the bottle, giving the wine a freshness and the faintest hint of 'sparkle', tangible but not visible.

The best Chianti is aged in cask, usually for at least five years, and bottled ready to drink. This wine, known as *Riserva*, is in a different class to other Chiantis and is one of Italy's finest wines.

South of Siena, but not in Chianti, is the village of Montalcino which makes a red wine from the Brunello grape. Brunello di Montalcino is an exceptional wine commanding very high prices. Strong, well-balanced, but needing time, this wine is one of the aristocrats of Italian vinification.

Still further south, and quite high in the Appenines is the old Etruscan town of Orvieto. From here come the white Orvietto secco and Orvietto Abbocato.

The latter is sweet and made from grapes which have been allowed to rot

Across to the east coast, near the town of Iesi, comes a very pleasant dry crisp white wine made from the Verdicchio grape and called Verdicchio del Castelli di Iesi.

From the area to the south of Rome comes a pleasant white wine, excellent with fish, called Frascati. From the north, near Montefiascone, comes a wine with the odd name of Est Est Est! – a sweet white wine. A story is told about a medieval German Bishop of Fulda who had been summoned to Rome, apparently for his misdeeds. The story relates that he sent his steward in advance to choose suitable inns, especially those with good wine, and to write on the door the latin word 'Est' meaning 'this is it' so that his master could recognise the inn of his choice. All went well during the journey across Europe until he arrived at Montefiascone where he found Est Est Est! because the steward had so liked the wine. The Bishop must have agreed with his manservant because he is said not to have progressed beyond Montefiascone and is buried in the local churchyard.

ITALIAN WINE & FOOD

Like France, Italy produces such a variety of wines that there is an abundance of choice for every dish. It has been said, a little unkindly, that Italian wine should only be consumed with Italian food. Given the range and versatility of Italian cooking, there seems to be nothing wrong with that notion, but Italian wines are deserving of much more attention internationally. The red wines of the north, the Barolos and Barberas of Piedmont, are ideally suited to red meats and game. Their strength, depth and richness is on a par with the "big" French wines of Hermitage and Châteauneuf-du-Pape. Many of Italy's vast assortment of dry white wines do not seem to be at all remarkable when tasted on their own, but as accompaniments to fish dishes, especially shellfish, they emerge as very sound wines. Soave, perhaps the best known Italian white wine, is seldom outstanding but is a very adaptable and attractive wine to drink with fish, pasta or white meats. Frascati is a wine to drink with the richer white meats, such as roast pork. Verdicchio, another wine commonly found outside Italy, is an excellent all-round table wine.

Southern Italy

South of Rome large quantities of robust red and white wines of high strength are made. Few of these are distinguished. Southern Italy has two volcanos which are still active, Vesuvius on the Bay of Naples and Etna in Sicily and the volcanic soil of the south influences some of the wine. Etna Bianco (white) and Corvo (both red and white) are excellent wines.

The best known wine of Sicily is undoubtedly Marsala, made famous by Nelson when his fleet was in the Mediterranean. The Marsala created by two English brothers, James and Woodhouse, is a rich fortified wine which may be dry or sweet. Drunk as an aperitif, Marsala is the Italian equivalent of Sherry but should not be compared with it – Marsala has a rich dark character of its own.

Lachryma Christi is a famous, and much exported wine, grown on the slopes of Vesuvius. At its best, the genuine article is a delicate golden sweet wine – ideally suited to the Mediterranean climate.

Ravello, both red and white, is one of the best wines of the south. The red is generally thought to be the better, but the white is decidedly more popular.

WINES FROM THE SOUTH

Making wine in hot, dry regions is a tricky business. In Italy, one must discover the names of the most reliable growers to be sure of good wine.

Leading growers
The Caruso family, whose grandiose labels, below, adorn bottles of the very best Ravello, make wine of all colours. Lacrima Christi, left, is a much imitated wine but Giuseppe Scala makes a very fine, genuine example.

SPAIN

Apart from Sherry, which is dealt with elsewhere in this book, Spain is notable for quantity rather than quality. On the whole, the climate is too hot and dry for fine wines and it is only in the more temperate northern parts that good wine is found. The rest of Spain has little of distinction to offer, and little of ordinary drinkable quality which cannot be bettered elsewhere. In Catalonia, particularly Pañades, there are some satisfying red wines – Sangre de Toro being the best. Valdepeñas is the name of most of the wines grown in La Mancha, the very centre of Spain. These wines are light, easy to drink, quite unexceptional and frequently served with the addition of ice, soda or brandy. Tarragona produces a very sweet fortified wine but it is in every way, inferior to Malaga – a once famous wine which is now rarely seen outside Spain. Malaga is similar to Marsala but more golden brown in colour.

The Rioja region

The red wines from Rioja, in Northern Castile, are among the very best in the world, yet they can be bought more easily and more cheaply than their counterparts in Bordeaux. It has been said that Riojas are the Claret and Burgundy of Spain. There is some truth in this: Riojas tend to come in two styles, dark and rich, light and fresh. The overall characteristics are of smoothness and the gentle ageing which comes from spending several years in barrel. Rioja is made in the way in which Claret was made in Bordeaux in the nineteenth century – ageing in oak being considered more important than ageing in glass. The best Riojas are the *Reservas*, but the ordinary wines never seem to fall below a good consistent quality and they are superb value – quite the best of all red wines.

Spain is not a notable producer of white wines, but the Rioja region does make a good one. The dry wine is much better than the sweet and has good ageing qualities. Indeed, the young wine can be rather hard. When mature, these wines have a golden colour and an instantly appealing scent.

The best recommendations for Portuguese wines can only be found in Portugal itself. No country in the world has such a range of satisfying, uncomplicated, country wines. In cafes and restaurants all over the country, the ordinary wine served at table will be better and cheaper than its counterparts in most other wine producing countries. Even outside Portugal, the wines are cheap but very few ever make it to the outside world. This is partly because many of the wines, especially the *Vinho Verde*, will not travel nor age well, and also because the wine trade in the main importing countries is slow to take up Portuguese wines.

Vinho Verde, which means 'green wine', is green in the sense of age rather than colour. The wine is bottled and sold very young and with a slight sparkle from a small degree of fermentation in the bottle.

The white *Vinho Verdes* are very simple wines but there are hundreds of them and only a few of the rather more sophisticated ones ever leave Portugal. They are excellent everyday wines and very easy to drink. The red equivalent, and most *Vinho Verde* are red, is rather strange wine – it looks like sparkling raspberry juice, and tastes not unlike it.

The best white wines of Portugal are called *maduro* – mature. They spend two years in barrel, on average, and are well cared for. Those from Bucelas and Dão are the best, but it will probably be necessary to look for brand names when buying this wine.

Portugal's finest red wine is Colares – a very dark and exceptionally long lasting wine which has some of the qualities of a good claret without really being like one.

The best known, and most reliable, red wine for everyday drinking which is available outside Portugal is Serradayres, but equally good wine will appear simply as Dão.

Unfortunately, the best as well as the worst of Portuguese wines are seldom exported, so the very fine *Reservas*, both white and red, will not be available to most readers of this book.

Most of the wine made in Hungary, Yugoslavia, Romania and Bulgaria is white – one of the few notable exceptions being Egri Bikaver, the famous Bull's Blood, from Hungary.

Hungary, whose wine-making tradition goes back further than the Austro-Hungarian empire, can also claim the best white wine in the eastern bloc. Tokay is one of the world's great sweet wines. It has a long and romantic history and the countryside in which it is made seems to come from the pages of a fairy story. It is, however, one of the world's most expensive wines.

Other Hungarian wines are well worth the drinking – they have a richness, fragrance and spiciness which is quite unique and not generally well-known. They are few and far between in other countries but by no means impossible to buy. Look for the wines from Badacsonyi and Mor.

Yugoslavian and Romanian wines are becoming more readily available. Generally, the Yugoslavian wines are the better – those coming from Macedonia can be very good indeed. Again, the quality wines are all white.

Romania produces a vast quantity of wine, much of which is exported, but there are many reasons to believe that the best of it stays at home. As in Yugoslavia, the Riesling makes the most reliable wine.

Bulgaria is another source of cheap, unexceptional wine, but better, and more original wine comes from the Soviet Union. Those from Georgia are the best.

PRODUCE OF YUGOSLAVIA

KVALITETNO VINO   QUALITY WINE

Hamnak

Single Vineyard   *Lutomer Laski Riesling*

GRAND GOLD MEDAL
AWARD WINNER

WORLD WINE EXHIBITION
LJUBLJANA 1976

e   SHIPPED & BOTTLED BY TELTSCHER BROTHERS LTD
60-66 TOOLEY STREET·LONDON SE1   68cl

Even if one were to attempt to gain an all-round appreciation of the world's wines it would still not be absolutely necessary to taste Swiss and Austrian wines. This is not to say that good wines are not produced in both countries – it is simply that better wines of the same type are produced elsewhere. Austria used to have some distinguished sweet wines but one would be hard pressed to find them today, although production of *Spätleses* and *Ausleses* in Burgenland, south of Vienna, has achieved some distinction in recent years.

The most famous wines of Greece are retsinas – retsina is not the name of a wine but an indication that the wine has had resin added during the fermentation. This practice was common 3000 years ago; whether it is continued for traditional or chemical reasons is not entirely clear. What seems fairly certain is that the wine is better with the resin than it would be without it. Among unresinated wines, the most commonly seen abroad are Mavrodaphne, a sweet red, and Pallini, a semi-sweet white.

Cyprus wines are very heady, perhaps the most powerful in the Northern hemisphere, but they have character and are improving all the time. That is to say, the methods of wine-making are improving. The best and most unique of Cyprus' wines is Commandaria – an immensely powerful syrup of a wine, but a real wine nonetheless. Commandaria is made from both red and white grapes.

In recent years (and we are talking of a wine growing industry whose history goes back little more than a hundred years), Californian wines have come to be taken seriously outside the USA. As a result, their exceptional quality has taken the world by surprise – or rather, it would if the wines were more easily obtainable. Californian wine-makers have become capable, using the Cabernet grape, of producing red wines as good as almost anything in Bordeaux. Unfortunately, the home market has a marked tendency to consume most of it, and long before it has matured. Like claret, Californian Cabernet needs time and is not able to show its true worth when young.

Wine growers in the Californian valleys are also successful with other European grapes, the Pinot Noir being next in importance to the Cabernet. They also have their own variety, the Zinfandel, which produces a light, fresh and slightly 'springy' wine. Blended wines are usually very good but there is no doubt that the Californian enthusiasm for single variety grapes is resulting in some very remarkable wines. The Napa Valley currently enjoys the reputation for the best Californian wines. Its Cabernet Sauvignon, Riesling and Chardonnay wines can be truly outstanding and it boasts an excellent 'Champagne'. More recently, the Salinas valley has become an important area of production. Some very fine wines are coming from the wineries of Paul Masson and Almaden. There is no doubt that, given time, the wines of California will be spoken of in the same breath as many of the finest European wines.

California
ZINFANDEL
Full-Bodied and Dry

A fine, hearty, full-bodied wine—deep red in color. One of the most versatile of red wines, Paul Masson's Zinfandel is a perfect companion to most dinner entrees. Serve at room temperature.

PAUL MASSON®

Alc.12% by Vol. * Paul Masson Vineyards, Saratoga, Ca., U.S.A. * *Made and bottled by* Contents 75 cl (e)

AUSTRALIA

The Australians who travel the world are quick to defend the reputation of the wine produced in their homeland. Indeed, they praise it to a degree which surprises those who have never tasted it. In fact, Australia not only makes excellent wine, but seems to find it easy to do so. It is such a vast country that it would be surprising not to find suitable wine growing land, but one would hardly expect the results that growers achieve with the Cabernet and Shiraz grapes. Australia makes white wine as well, good wine, using the Riesling grape but in nothing like the quantity of the red wines.

Hugh Johnson has said that Australia is capable of making some of the world's greatest red wine. Unfortunately, very few people outside Australia are able to share this view because most of the best wines are not exported and there is a vast difference between the best and the average.

SOUTH AMERICA

Most South American wine is not high quality. Argentina, Brazil and Uruguay all produce considerable quantities of wine, and Argentina is beginning to find an export market, but the South American country with most to offer is Chile.

The Chilean wine industry, like the Californian and Australian, makes great use of the Cabernet grape and uses similar methods to make their red wines to those employed in Bordeaux. The wines exhibit many of the qualities of Claret and are equally long-living. Chilean white wines should not be overlooked, the use of Sauvignon and Riesling grapes is producing very characterful wine. As in many of the countries whose wine industries are just beginning to find external markets, South American wines invariably declare the grape variety on the label. This practise is extremely helpful to those familiar only with European wine.

FORTIFIED AND DESSERT WINES

There are more fortified wines in the world than can be comfortably dealt with in the pages of this book. What follows is a selection of the best and the best known, together with one or two that are deserving of more international attention.

Sherry

Fine sherry comes from the Jerez region of southern Spain, just above the Straits of Gibraltar. The region takes its name from the town of Jerez or, to give it its full name, Jerez de la Frontera. In ancient times it was the frontier town between the Christian occupied north and the Moorish occupied south, until reunited under the Christian Kingdom after the expulsion of the Moors.

The wines of the region have been known outside Spain for many centuries. In fact, Sir Francis Drake, (El Draco to the Spanish), when he sacked the town of Cadiz confiscated some 3000 casks of Sherry from the Quay, and took them home. There are also many references to Sherris and Sherris Sack in Shakespearian works; the wine however must have been quite different from the Sherry of today because it was not fortified.

Sherry today is a quite unique wine and can range from very pale and very dry to very dark and very sweet. It is, however, a white wine and produced from a single grape variety – the Palomino – with just a few subsidiary varieties for the sweeter wines. The hot climate in southern Spain, together with the rather chalky soil, produces grapes very high in sugar which convert into a wine with a very high natural alcohol content 14% or more. The chalky soil is responsible for a rather noticeable acidity in the wine. It is these features that that produce one of the most popular styles: the dry Fino and Manzanilla Sherries. Besides the unique climate and soil conditions, the methods of sherry production are quite unique, the style of maturation and manufacture differing greatly from other wine producing regions.

Generic Sherries

Other sherries are produced in South Africa, Australia and Cyprus. Of these, South African is closest to the sherry from Jerez. South African producers use the Palomino grape, just as they do in Spain, and they have the good fortune that *Flor* grows on some of their wines – with the result that some very good and very 'Spanish' wines appear.

Australian sherry has improved immensely in recent years. Many of the drier styles are produced on a *Flor* system, but the rather hotter climate of Australia does tend to give the wines a style which lacks some of the finesse of both Jerez and South African sherries.

How Sherry is made

The grapes, which are always white, are picked as they would be in any wine producing region and taken to the press house where they are pressed and put into the fermentation vessels. Fermentation is unique in that it is very tumultuous at first. It is said that as much as 98% of the alcohol is converted in the first 48 to 50 hours. The fermentation continues for 50 days at a much slower and quieter rate.

The new young wine is then sent to the *Bodegas* (Bodegas are large church-like warehouses, the equivalent of a cellar but above ground) and the start of the maturation cycle begins. The young wines are lightly fortified, and during the early stage of their maturation a unique phenomenon takes place. On some of the wines a yeast-like substance called *Flor* settles on the top of the wine in the casks; only these wines will develop into the Fino Manzanilla and Amontillado sherries. The wines on which *Flor* does not grow will develop from the early *rayas* stage into the Olorosos and some of them will become cream sherry. The *Flor* and non *Flor* wines are classified into their separate groups and these are fed into what is called the Solera system.

The Solera System

The purpose of this system is to achieve an absolutely constant method of blending – one that ensures that the shipper can always produce a bottle of Sherry identical to the last.

The method is lengthy and labour intensive, there being many stages to go through. The new wine, called the *Añada* (wine of the year), is added to a wine of the same type but one stage more mature. The process continues throughout the stages of maturation so that each cask is being topped up by the next oldest. Ultimately a mature wine of the designated style is drawn from the oldest barrel. Even then, further blending is required to achieve the necessary style required by the market. Very few unblended Sherries, known as straight soleras, are ever sold and they are very expensive. The reason for all this blending is that Sherry is naturally the driest drink on earth and in unmodified form would find few takers.

Even straight soleras tend to be too dry for most tastes and so nearly all of the proprietary blends which are sold by wine merchants and supermarkets have had sweetening and colouring wines added in the final stages.

RECOGNIZING SHERRIES

Fino
A very dry, pale Sherry. Even these have usually been sweetened but they are the nearest you can get to unblended Sherry – except in Spain. The ideal aperitif.

Manzanilla
Pale, delicate Sherry which sometimes has a slightly salty tang. The saltiness is said to come from the sea air at Sanlúcar de Barrameda where the wine is stored. Unfortunately, it loses this tang when shipped.

Amontillado
A fatter and fuller fino, matured to become darker and stronger. Some commercial brands of mid-brown, sweetish Sherry use the name amontillado, but they have little in common with the real thing.

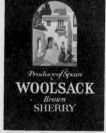

Oloroso
These wines stay in cask for a long time and live to a great age. Many of them are used in blending the richest, darkest and sweetest Sherries.

Milk
A smooth, silky Sherry, gentle and sweet. This term was first used in Bristol during the great days of the wine trade

Cream
This has all the qualities of Milk Sherry but, as its name suggests, is smoother and richer. It is also somewhat older.

Brown
Brown Sherry is not very often seen these days. It is very dark, sweet and has a stickiness and flavour which is almost treacly.

Montilla

Montilla is a region 100 miles or so further inland than Jerez; its wine has many of the characteristics of sherry but with one very important difference – it is an unfortified wine.

Montilla has been overshadowed by its big brother for many, many years but now it is asserting its authority and becoming better known outside Spain. The principal grape variety is the Pedro Ximenez, which is used in Jerez for sweetening. The soil, too, has many characteristics being composed of chalky albariza and lime marl. The hotter inland climate results in a very much higher sugar content in the grapes than in Jerez, and therefore produces a natural alcohol level somewhere between 15% and 18% after fermentation. Fermentation takes place in large earthenware jars called tinajars which look a bit like huge ink wells. It is then transferred to oak casks or tanks, after which it is fed through a Solera system not unlike that used in Jerez.

During the maturation process Flor will grow on some of the wines and these will become very light, dry Montillas in the style of Fino sherries – the fuller wines developing like the Amontillado sherries. The word Amontillado means 'like Montilla', and cannot, therefore, be used as a description for Montilla wines, it would be a bit like saying 'a wine like a wine like a wine that comes from Montilla' when it came from Montilla in the first place.

For the sweet Montillas, the Pedro Ximenez grapes are laid out in the sun to dehydrate and so concentrate the sugar. Many experts contend that the sweet Montillas are frequently better than some of the cream sherries because they have a rounder, more natural taste – brought about by the naturally high alcohol level. Montilla has often been referred to as the poor man's sherry – perhaps an unfair description because the wine has its own rather individual status. In economic terms, however, there is some justification for the comment, Montilla is somewhat cheaper than the comparable sherries.

Port

In northern Portugal, among the Douro mountains and along the upper reaches of the Douro river, grow the vines which give the world one of its most revered wines. Port, as an unfortified wine, would be remarkable only for its blackish colour and unpalatable taste. Its secret lies in fortification and blending. That the grapes which provide the base wine should contain the qualities which, after years of maturation, will become apparent in the wine, is nothing short of incredible.

In the upper Douro there is almost no soil: the heavy shistous surface which is a combination of compressed clay and granite, and the steep hillsides combine to form land which is most unfavourable to the grape. The climate, also, is extreme. In this region, close to the Spanish border and cut off from the influence of the Atlantic by mountains, summers are extremely hot with temperatures commonly exceeding 38°C (100°F). In winter, up to 127cm (50ins) of rain may fall, much of which would just run off the slopes were it not for the e.iborate terracing which the Port growers have built. The terracing, which is being constantly extended into new areas and unplanted tributaries of the Douro, has enabled the formation of soil but, even so, it is sometimes necessary to use explosives to break the ground before planting.

From this extraordinary land come the Port grapes – 30 or 40 varieties of them – which are still trodden by teams of men in a cement trough called a *lagar*. Fermentation takes place in the growers farm, or *quinta*. The young, partially fermented wine is run into barrels which are quarter-filled with brandy. This stops the fermentation, strengthens the wine and preserves a considerable proportion of the natural sugar. No sweetening is ever added to Port.

The wine is then taken down to Oporto where the shippers, many of whom have their own *quintas*, store the wine in oak barrels called *pipes*.

Blending Port

Wines which are readily available in most stores, ports for everyday drinking, are blended wines. The non-vintage wine is kept in its pipes for anything up to 40 or 50 years and the degree of blending and maturing which takes place during its storage determines the type of wine it will be. Ruby port is the youngest. It may be four or five years old when it reaches the wine merchants and stores. It is a blend of new and old wines, but as a blend it is still young. Tawny port is also a blend but one that has received several years more maturation than ruby. Tawny is the colour it becomes as it fades during storage in the oak barrels. Very old tawny is a remarkable wine, beautifully smooth and finely balanced. It is a good deal more expensive than young tawny or ruby, but it is incomparably the better drink.

White port, made from white grapes is an excellent aperitif being drier than other ports.

Late bottled vintage is wine from good years that has been left in barrel, unblended, for up to seven years. If it is bottled at that age the crust or sediment which is always formed in vintage port will be left in the barrel at bottling.

VINTAGE PORT

In years when conditions have been absolutely right for making port, the shippers may declare a vintage. This is entirely a matter of individual choice – there are no rules – but when a vintage is declared, the wine will be bottled at two years and left to mature for as much as 20 years and more.

RECENT VINTAGES	
1975	Not a big vintage, but good
1970	Very good; ready for drinking in early 1980's
1967	Light vintage; ready to drink now
1966	Very big; excellent wines can be drunk now but will repay keeping
1963	One of the truly great vintages; fetching high prices now
1960	Another big vintage; drinking well now

1963
Vintage Port

SHIPPED BY
SOC. AGRÍCOLA E COMERCIAL DOS VINHOS MESSIAS
S.A.R.L.
V. N. DE GAIA   PORTUGAL

Madeira

Madeira has at various times been one of the most fashionable of drinks and one of the most neglected. In Victorian times it was in its heyday, both as an aperitif and as an after dinner wine. Today, after something of a lull in interest, it is regaining some of its old popularity.

The wine produced on the island of Madeira is unexceptional, but it is put through a rather curious process which can only be described as 'cooking' and this results in a wine which is instantly mature and very long lasting.

Madeira is blended, by the Solera system, and fortified with brandy, but its unique characteristics come from the 90 days the wine spends in heated vats at a temperature of 49°C (120°F). This has the effect of concentrating the process of maturation, which would otherwise be absurdly long, into a very short period and ensures that the wine is absolutely stable. It can, therefore, be shipped to any part of the world without losing any of its characteristics. This extraordinary process is known as *maderisation*. Madeira is available at prices which make it very hard to understand why it is a comparatively neglected wine.

Setúbal

One other rich dessert wine from Portugal is worthy of mention here. This is the wine of Setúbal near Lisbon in the south of Portugal. This luscious, rich white wine is, like port, made by arresting the fermentation: so concentrating some of the original grape sugar

Moscatel de Setúbal is made with Muscatel grapes of two varieties, one of them black, although it is the white which is used in greater quantities. After the fermentation has been arrested with brandy, the wine is left to mature but with the addition of some Muscatel grape skins which are left in the wine to enhance the flavour and bouquet until the spring racking. It is a wine that matures and ages exceptionally well, retaining the wonderful Muscatel fragrance and gaining a deeper golden amber colour with age.

For some reason, Setúbal is not a well-known or fashionable wine – perhaps modern taste discriminate against it as it does many of the unfortified sweet wines – but its price suggests that popularity could be only just around the corner. Wines which are twenty-five years old are fairly easy to find and will cost far less than any comparable wine of similar maturity.

Marsala

The wine of Marsala, produced at the far western tip of the Island of Sicily, is undoubtedly the island's most famous wine. Originally it was the product of an Englishman, John Woodhouse, who realised that the conditions in this part of Sicily were capable of producing a wine not unlike port or Madeira. Woodhouse, with his brother, set up business and started to export the wines, but it was Admiral Lord Nelson who really made it famous when he purchased quite large quantities to victual the Mediterranean Fleet under his command. The wine is not unlike Madeira in that it is fortified and that certain parts of it go through a heating process.

Marsala is made by adding to the local, rather heavy, white wine of the district brandy, some sweeter wine made from semi-dried grapes and then some unfermented grape juice which has been heated slowly until it has become quite thick, caramel-like in colour and texture. This mixture is matured for up to five years, during which time it becomes quite dark in colour – although originally it was a white wine. Some of the finer wine might be matured on a Solera system similar to that used for sherry.

GREEN ISLAND WINES

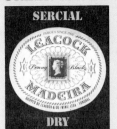

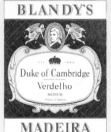

The richly fertile volcanic island which we call Madeira makes little natural wine worthy of consideration but its fortified wines are unique. There are four main types of Madeira the names of which are derived from grape varieties.

Sercial is the lightest and the driest of Madeiras and is the most suitable for drinking as an aperitif. It has quite a distinct tang and a surprising freshness.

Verdelho is sweeter than Sercial, richer, fruitier and more acid. A very smooth alternative to either sherry or port.

Bual is sweet enough to suit most palates as a dessert wine, rich but not heavy and still having the characteristic Madeira freshness.

Malmsey is the sweetest, darkest, richest and most caramelised of the Madeiras. One of the great dessert wines.

Glossary of terms

Acidity
Wine contains several types of acid, including tartaric acid, citric acid and malic acid. The function of acid in wine is to maintain a balance between the fruit and the alcohol.

Appellation contrólee
The French system of controlling and regulating wine production, applies to the top 20% of wines.

Bereich
German word applied to a district including many vineyards.

Blanc de blancs
Wine made only from white grapes, but from more than one variety.

Body
A word used by wine tasters to denote mouth filling sensations and depth.

Bouquet
A complex mixture of smells which develop as the wine matures. Scent, fragrance and aroma are all part of the bouquet.

Bourgeois
A category of Bordeaux wines applied to individual vineyards just below "classed" growth status.

Brut
Means 'dry', and is chiefly used to describe the driest Champagnes and sparkling wines.

Cepage
A French word referring to grape variety.

Cru
The word means 'growth', but is usually only applied when indicating the particular classification of the wine, e.g. *Grand Cru Classé*.

Cuvée
The contents of a vat. Some expressions, such as Premier Cuvée and Tête de Cuvée, are used to denote superior wine.

Demi-sec
Not half-dry, or semi-dry, as many might suppose, but well on the way to being sweet.

DOC
The Italian system of quality control.

Faded
A wine which has lost its chief characteristics, wholly or partially, is said to have faded. Usually, but not necessarily, applied to old wines.

Fortification
The process of adding brandy to natural wines to stop fermentation, preserve some of the natural sugar and boost the alcohol content.

Green
A word used to describe the qualities of youth and freshness in wine. It can be applied to mature wines which have those characteristics.

Claret
The English word used to denote red Bordeaux wine.

Climats

The term used in Burgundy to describe an individual grower's vineyard or portion of vineyards.

Clos

Strictly speaking, an enclosed vineyard, not necessarily belonging to one grower.

Corked

A serious fault, not resulting from the vinification process, but from a defective cork. The defect may develop long after bottling, and manifest itself in a variety of ways. The wine may be odourless and completely flat, or it may have an unpleasant 'chemical' smell.

Côte

Means 'slope'. Much used in France to denote areas of vineyards. *Coteaux* means 'hillsides'.

Hock

An English word, derived from *Hocheim*, used to describe Rhein wines.

Maderisation

The process of oxidation which produces a brownish colour in some wines – so that they bear a resemblance to Madeira.

Noble Rot

Botrytis cinerea, which dehydrates the grape and concentrates the sugar. Essential in the making of Sauternes and other naturally sweet wines.

Nose

Closely related to 'bouquet', this applies to the immediate impression made by the wine on the nose of the taster.

Oxidation

The deterioration of wine as a result of exposure to the air. Produces some very unpleasant smells and tastes.

Pétillant

A slight sparkle, sometimes called 'prickle' which can make white wines pleasantly uplifting. It is due to a degree of fermentation in the bottle, and should not be approved in red wine.

Sulphur

Sulphur dioxide is much used in wine making to kill unwanted bacteria. There is nothing wrong with its use but it must be carefully controlled or the wine will smell of sulphur and irritate the palate and throat.

Tannin

A substance derived from the skins and stalks of grapes which helps to prolong the life of the wine. All of the very substantial and long-lived red wines have it.

Tough

One of the qualities of young wine, especially those which have a high tannin content. Not an unacceptable feature.

VDQS

The second level of quality control in France, accounting for about 5% of wine.

Index

Acknowledgments

The 'How To' Book of Choosing
and Enjoying Wine was created
by Simon Jennings and Company
Limited. We are grateful to
the following individuals and
organisations for their assistance
in the making of this book:

Stephen Bull: *design and drawing of maps*
John Couzins: *cover and title page photographs, and pages 22–3*
Ann Hall: *compilation of index*
Jackson Day Designs: *line illustrations*
The Dover Archive: *engravings and embellishments*
Carole Johnson: *line illustrations*
Susan Milne: *colour illustrations*
Dee Robinson: *picture research*
The Scolar Press: *engravings and embellishments*
Helena Zakrsewska-Rucinska: *hand tinting of engravings*

Photographs:
British Library: page **7** *t* and *bl*
British Museum: pages **6** *b*; **9**
Robert Harding Associates: pages **19** *t*; **26** *b*; **27** *r*; **31**
Hedges and Butler: pages **6** *t*; **7** *br*; **10** *t* and *b*; **II**
International Distillers and Vinters: pages **18** *t*; **26** *t*; **27** *bl*
Mentzendorff and Co.: page **62**
Moet and Chandon: pages **30***t* and *b*; **31** *bl*
Wine and Food From France: page **18** *b*
Wine and Spirit Education Trust: page **27** *c*
ZEFA: pages **14**; **19** *bl*

abbreviations: *t* top; *b* bottom; *c* centre; *tl* top left; *tr* top right;
bl bottom left; *br* bottom right; *r* right

Typesetting by Servis Filmsetting Ltd., Manchester
Headline setting by Facet Photosetting, London

Special thanks to Norman Ruffell and
the staff of Swaingrove Ltd., Bury St. Edmunds,
Suffolk, for the lithographic reproduction.

'HOW TO'